New Library of Pastoral Care
GENERAL EDITOR: DEREK BLOWS

Meaning in Madness

Titles in this series include:

Still Small Voice: An Introduction to Counselling
MICHAEL JACOBS

Letting Go: Caring for the Dying and Bereaved
PETER SPECK AND IAN AINSWORTH-SMITH

Living Alone: The Inward Journey to Fellowship
MARTIN ISRAEL

Invisible Barriers: Pastoral Care with Physically Disabled People
JESSIE VAN DONGEN-GARRAD

Learning to Care: Christian Reflection on Pastoral Practice
MICHAEL H. TAYLOR

Liberating God: Private Care and Public Struggle
PETER SELBY

Make or Break: An Introduction to Marriage Counselling
JACK DOMINIAN

Meaning in Madness: The Pastor and the Mentally Ill
JOHN FOSKETT

Paid to Care?: The Limits of Professionalism in Pastoral Care
ALASTAIR V. CAMPBELL

New Library of Pastoral Care
GENERAL EDITOR: DEREK BLOWS

MEANING IN MADNESS

The Pastor and the Mentally Ill

John Foskett

First published 1984
SPCK
Holy Trinity Church
Marylebone Road
London NW1 4DU

British Library Cataloguing in Publication Data

Foskett, John
Meaning in madness.
1. Church work with the mentally ill.
2. Pastoral counselling
I. Title
259'.4 BV4461

ISBN 0-281-04128-8

Filmset by Pioneer
Printed in Great Britain by
the Anchor Press, Tiptree

To
Mary, Andrew, Tim, Sam and Naomi
for loving me
'madness and all'

Contents

Foreword

The *New Library of Pastoral Care* has been planned to meet the needs of those people concerned with pastoral care, whether clergy or lay, who seek to improve their knowledge and skills in this field. Equally, it is hoped that it may prove useful to those secular helpers who may wish to understand the role of the pastor.

Pastoral care in every age has drawn from contemporary secular knowledge to inform its understanding of man and his various needs and of the ways in which these needs might be met. Today it is perhaps the secular helping professions of social work, counselling and psychotherapy, and community development which have particular contributions to make to the pastor in his work. Such knowledge does not stand still, and a pastor would have a struggle to keep up with the endless tide of new developments which pour out from these and other disciplines, and to sort out which ideas and practices might be relevant to his particular pastoral needs. Among present-day ideas, for instance, of particular value might be an understanding of the social context of the pastoral task, the dynamics of the helping relationship, the attitudes and skills as well as factual knowledge which might make for effective pastoral intervention, and perhaps most significant of all, the study of particular cases, whether through verbatim reports of interviews or general case presentation. The discovery of ways of learning from what one is doing is becoming increasingly important.

There is always a danger that a pastor who drinks deeply at the well of a secular discipline may lose his grasp of his own pastoral identity and become 'just another' social worker or counsellor. It in no way detracts from the value of these professions to assert that the role and task of the pastor are quite unique among the helping professions and deserve to be clarified and strengthened rather than weakened. The theological commitment of the pastor and the appropriate use of his role will be a recurrent theme of the series. At the same time the pastor cannot afford to work in a vacuum. He needs to be able to communicate and co-operate with those helpers in other disciplines whose work may overlap, without loss of his own unique role. This in turn will mean being able to communicate with them through some understanding of their concepts and language.

Finally, there is a rich variety of styles and approaches in pastoral work within the various religious traditions. No attempt will be made to secure a uniform approach. The Library will contain the variety, and even perhaps occasional eccentricity, which such a title suggests. Some books will be more specifically theological and others more concerned with particular areas of need or practice. It is hoped that all of them will have a usefulness that will reach right across the boundaries of religious denomination.

DEREK BLOWS
Series Editor

Acknowledgements

Writing about important matters is never easy. The written word rarely does justice to that which it seeks to express. I suppose that is why Christianity is an incarnate faith more than it is a verbal one. 'Madness' is an important matter. Words about it are not adequate even to capture its mysteries let alone to reveal its meaning. To understand it one has, incarnate like, to enter into it – into one's own and other people's madness. It is my experience and conviction that there is meaning to be found there; inadequate as the words of this book are, I hope they will convey something of it. In so far as they do, it will be due to the generosity of all who knowingly or unwittingly have contributed to my search and so to my experience and conviction. I am especially grateful to all those people in the parishes, diocese and hospitals where I have worked, to my friends and colleagues and most of all to my family; to the pastors and to Pam, Joan, Emma, Ray, Edward, Sarah, David, Leslie, Mary, Harry, and the members of 'Faith and Doubt' (whose names and some personal details only have been changed, for obvious reasons), who encouraged me to let their stories and their experiences illuminate my own. As one who was obviously dyslexic before that word was coined, I owe a special debt of gratitude to Mary Foskett, Cathy Crawford and Joy Wright, who in typing many manuscripts confronted my ambivalence for words, particularly the written kind. Finally I should like to thank Diana Wallis for her occupational therapy programmes which so often rehabilitated my waning confidence, Stuart Checkley for his help with Chapter 7, and Derek Blows with whom I wrestled like Jacob at Penuel, and shared both the pain and the blessing of this enterprise.

JOHN FOSKETT

Part One

ONE

Introduction

The history of the relationship between religion and psychiatry is a mixed one, and consequently the followers of both approach each other with some caution and suspicion. Nevertheless they do share some things in common, like their enmity against what each regards as unacceptable. The former fights with sin, while the latter attacks suffering. The fact that neither has been conspicuously successful in eliminating either of their adversaries may well have led both to consider alternative approaches. In psychiatry the simple and single-minded attack upon the symptoms of suffering is tempered by a more careful examination for the psychological as well as the physiological causes of those symptoms. In religion there has been a revival of interest in those aspects of the Judaeo/Christian tradition which are not so exclusively opposed to evil in general or to sin in particular. The worst in human experience is seen to have meaning and value after all, as it did in the exile and the crucifixion. There is an alternative somewhere between a stoical acceptance of, and a hostile attack upon, sin and suffering. They can be embraced as but one side of a coin whose other face will reveal salvation and health.

Pastoral care as a whole and pastoral counselling in particular have enabled helper and helped to test this alternative against reality. Carers and counsellors have drawn upon the behavioural sciences as well as theology in their search for the meaning, not of suffering in general, but of the specific sufferings of individuals and groups. In Part One of this book readers are invited to look at suffering from this point of view; to eavesdrop on the conversations of counsellors and counselled, to reflect with pastors upon the revelations of their work, and to hear directly what it is like to suffer a mental illness. In Part Two different perspectives are explored separately. Counsellors need to know about themselves, their motives, strengths and weaknesses, if they are to help rather than harm their clients. Psychiatry, counselling and theology all have different contributions to make, and different limitations which need to be recognized. Because 'madness' is such an enigma, it can so easily separate helper from helped, and isolate one discipline from another. Writing about mental illness in the last century Connelly had this to say about the importance of the relationship of physician and pastor:

> It affords the resident phsyician much satisfaction to be able to say that the kind and judicious co-operation of the Chaplain, and his frequent and unreserved communications, are such as to inspire him with the fullest confidence . . . Long experience can alone determine the cases to which religious attentions are applicable; they are sometimes beneficial where the advantage was scarcely hoped for, and sometimes excite when no excitement was expected . . . Nothing can meet the various difficulties incidental to such delicate trials, except the constant and confidential communications of the physician and chaplain to each other. If the physician may sometimes prevent mischief that might arise from an ill-timed religious appeal, the chaplain is sometimes enabled by his intercourse with the patients to demonstrate that the influence of his spiritual conversation is deeper and more permanent than the physician might expect.[1]

This book is written for all whose life or work is touched by the mystery of 'madness', physicians and chaplains, patients and professional health workers, relatives and friends, pastors and counsellors — for all who want encouragement to find some meaning in 'madness'.

Notes

1. Connelly, J., *The Hanwell Asylum Report,* 1841, p. 237.

TWO

Counselling Individuals

Introduction

In this chapter, a number of pastors, men and women (variously referred to as priests, ministers and hospital chaplains), record conversations they had while learning about the pastoral care of the mentally ill. These appear, as they were remembered and recorded by the pastors, on left-hand pages, and on the opposite pages are the reactions, comments and suggestions that arose when the pastors discussed their work with colleagues in a supervisory meeting. There are a number of important assumptions implied in this kind of presentation.

In this book, pastoral care is used as a general term to encompass a number of activities – caring, teaching, managing and directing, as well as counselling. The ordinary exchanges between pastor and pastored are the raw material of pastoral care. It is the aim of this chapter to concentrate on the counselling (hence the term pastoral counselling),[1] which was beginning to be fashioned out of that material with the help of supervision.

All helping requires both doing or trying to do, and thinking about what has been done and what might be done in future. The activity of pastoral care is not in itself enough to enable us to learn when and how to counsel. We need the opportunity and the help to think about what we have done and said, about what we thought and felt, what we would like to do and say in the future, and how best to go about it. This reflection, consideration and preparation is the work of supervision, a well-known procedure in social work and counselling for instance, but still relatively new to pastors.

Of course there is a difference between the spontaneous comments of ordinary conversation and those 'counselling' responses which pastors are encouraged to make in order to be helpful. In a later chapter the reasons for this will be explained in greater detail.[2] It may, however, help if the reader understands the following:

1. Counsellors aim to convey their readiness just to be with the person seeking help and to try to understand them, their feelings as well as their thoughts and problems.

2. Counsellors endeavour to suspend their judgement about what has been said or felt, so as not to be inadvertent censors of anything that needs expressing. They suspend judgement, not in order to condone, but in order to understand and to help their counsellees understand themselves better.

3. Counsellors will be particularly sensitive to how a conversation begins, develops and ends. They will note what is difficult for the counsellor and the counselled when, for instance, either of them diverts or redirects the course of the conversation. This assumes that the 'process' is as indicative of what is important as the 'content' of a conversation.

4. Counsellors will be attentive to how they themselves feel, and will endeavour to make use of those feelings as clues to how their counsellees may be feeling.

5. Counsellors work on the assumption that the way they behave and what they do conveys as much if not more than what they say.

It is not easy for pastors inexperienced in counselling to maintain responses built upon these assumptions, to make them in a natural and personal way, and to maintain them under the stress of what they hear and feel as the conversation develops. Pastors, like other helpers, retreat in the face of the demands which helping makes upon them. Retreating can take the form of looking on the lighter side, explaining or arguing away difficulties, defending oneself or one's beliefs and, for pastors especially, talking about or praying to God. Supervision is the arena in which the skills of pastoral counselling can be learnt, developed and made personal to the individual pastor. In the conversations which follow, it will be clear that much attention is given in supervision to what has gone wrong, and to the pastor's feelings of not doing very well. This is because our failures in helping so often provide the richest material for our growth and development as pastoral counsellors. After all, those who seek our help come not because of their sucesses but because of their failures and their difficulties. Nothing could be more important to them than to find that such things are the very foundation of the growth and development which they seek.[3]

Learning to counsel

Each of the pastoral relationships recorded below is, of course, unique and any generalization drawn from them should not be allowed to detract from that uniqueness. Nevertheless, the order in which they are presented follows a sequence. Pam has no history of mental illness when she comes to see her minister, but like many who turn to their pastors she is worried by her strange feelings and wants support in order to find, and then accept, help. She highlights the stigma associated with 'madness' and what a difficult hurdle that is to negotiate. Joan and Emma are both patients in a psychiatric hospital, because they could no longer manage their lives at home. Emma's unresolved grief and Joan's despair with herself have each taken their toll. All three would be described as suffering from a neurotic illness, that is to say, they are in touch with reality and are all too aware of the problems which cause their illness.[4] Ray is in a different position; he has been in prison as well as in hospital, and his problem is that he fits nowhere, and so, like many others, he is said to have a personality disorder.[5] Edward and Sarah exhibit more closely the stereotype of 'madness'. Their contact with external reality is fragile, and is easily overwhelmed by the chaos of a more pressing inner reality that is mostly unavailable to those who try to help them. Their illnesses are normally described as psychotic, and they require a very particular and exact use of the counsellor's skill.[6]

Pam

Pam is a middle-aged lady, a regular member of a local congregation. She approached her minister in some distress and asked if she could talk to him. He arranged an appointment for her at which the following conversation takes place.

MINISTER: Hello, Pam, do come in and make yourself comfortable. Would you like some coffee? 1

PAM: Yes please.
(They talk about the parish while he prepares the coffee. Then she falls silent, and he waits for her to begin. When she cannot, he speaks.)

MINISTER: You were very distressed when I saw you in church on Sunday. 2

PAM: I was, that's why I wanted to come and see you. I was upset during the sermon. *(She pauses and looks anxiously at him.)*

Pam

How to begin

A great deal is achieved in this short beginning. First the minister has taken trouble to prepare himself and Pam for something that he guessed would not be easy. He has set aside time and a safe place for their talk, so conveying to Pam that she has his undivided attention, and his confidentiality. In our hurrying we often allow conversations to happen in unsuitable places, and by failing to set a time for them, expose ourselves and others to the anxiety of not knowing when and how to stop.

Safety versus neutrality

1 The minister encourages Pam to make herself comfortable, and busies himself with making coffee and talking generally. By so doing he allows her to relax and feel the security of this relationship. It is not easy to strike the right balance of neutrality. An overwarm welcome, or a very cool one, hinders a person getting down to what they want to say. For instance, people who feel angry or frightened are not helped if they are greeted with the kind of excessive warmth which steels their anger.

In this case the minister has allowed some silence to give Pam the chance to start as she wants.

2 When he sees that she is unable to, he helps her by recalling her previous distress. Alternatively, he could have said something about the difficulty she was having in trying to begin. 'It is one thing to ask to come and see me, Pam, but I sense that it is another thing, to know how to start talking about what is troubling you.' Such a response speaks directly to Pam's unexpressed feelings, so giving her permission not to find it easy to begin. It reveals to her a pastor, who is prepared to be with her in her uncertainty and fear.

MINISTER: What upset you, Pam? 3

PAM: It was as if you were preaching directly to me. Just as though you were getting at me. It upset me very much.

MINISTER: Has this happened before? 4

PAM: It happens at work. *(Silence.)*

MINISTER: It happens at work, Pam? 5

PAM: Yes, I get this feeling that people are talking about me. When I go into the office they all stop talking, and I know they are talking about me. Some time ago some money was missing where I work, and I felt that everyone thought I had taken it.

MINISTER: And what made you think that? 6

PAM: I don't know, I just did. I was so upset, my husband went to see the manager, and he assured him that I had nothing to do with it. My husband keeps telling me that I'm imagining it, and that it is all in my mind. But I know these things happen, people do talk about me. . . Do you think I imagine it all?

3 Pam explains what upset her, she thought the minister's sermon was addressed to her. To hear that we have upset someone by what we have said or done is usually enough to make us recoil, and perhaps Pam feared that reaction to her implied criticism. As we recoil, we are prone to defend or justify ourselves, to explain away or make better our discomfort; but by doing so we run the risk of cutting short what needs to be said. The minister does not do this directly, but 4 indirectly he diverts the conversation from his sermon, to her distress in some other context. 'Has this happened before?' He might have said, 'I can imagine how disturbing it was to feel that I was talking directly to you, was there something in particular I said that upset you, or was it the way I said it?'

The art of reflection

5 Having diverted the conversation the minister gently encourages Pam to say more by repeating her brief answer. This is a good example of how the very simplest of reflections, repeating the words she has said, is enough to help her go on. As she does her anxiety begins to take shape. What is even more important it takes the shape she gives it, and not one fashioned by the minister's questions.

6 Her anxiety has two aspects to it. First, she is convinced that people talk about her and blame her. That is worrying enough but, secondly, she fails to get her experience corroborated by others. They make her doubt her conviction and so doubt herself. She is sinking deeper into a quicksand of doubt and suspicion, and her question to the minister is the cry of someone drowning.

MINISTER: It all seems very real to you, Pam, and I can understand that you are very distressed. 7

PAM: My husband says that I should see my doctor. I saw him some time ago, and he gave me some tablets to calm me down. I did feel a little better for a time. Do you think I should go and see him again?

MINISTER: Do you think you should see him again? 8

PAM: I don't know. *(There follows a long silence during which Pam is very distressed.)* My children are beginning to feel that something is wrong. Perhaps I ought to see my doctor and explain just how I feel. *(She pauses and seems to be struggling with this decision; then she says with a sudden relief:)* I feel much better having talked to you.

MINISTER: Thank you for sharing this with me.

7 Once again the minister is faced with a dilemma. Should he take sides or throw her a lifebelt of reassurance? In fact the minister does something better still, he is not panicked by her, and he is able to speak again directly to her concern. It is all very real to Pam; whether she is objectively right or wrong about her experience is irrelevant at this moment. Her anxiety obscures everything else, and it is that which the minister acknowledges and so holds, metaphorically, in his hands. There is nothing so essential to effective pastoral care as the pastor's ability to convey a willingness to be with and stay with the experience of the pastored, however disturbing or confusing that experience turns out to be.[7]

Learning to trust oneself

8 The minister's presence beside Pam is an unspoken encouragement for her to explore further. By not answering her question himself and by conveying his interest in her answers, he allows her to rediscover her capacity to cope with what is happening. Her problem is not solved but she has regained some of her confidence, and that will help her make a better job of explaining her difficulties to the doctor. What is more, she now has the companionship of someone who she knows understands or, at least, will work hard to understand her. Until now she has felt isolated from others because their experience and hers always seemed to be different and in conflict. That is why she feels better for having talked to the minister. He has not answered the question about her sanity, but she now knows that it is that question which, quite naturally, worries her most. Her minister might have helped her more by saying something to that effect. 'I see how difficult it is for you to decide about seeing a doctor. So much hangs upon it, and you're not sure whether he will understand.' On the other hand, his sympathetic silence gives her the chance to decide for herself.

Joan

Joan is in her early sixties, a patient in a psychogeriatric unit because of a severe depression. This has been heightened because her doctor has withdrawn her medication in order to identify what it is that is causing Joan such distress. Joan is angry and hurt by the hospital's policy, but is also beginning to talk more openly about herself. The student chaplain, in this case a woman, had the following conversation with her.

JOAN: I see you are a student chaplain. Does that mean you go round talking to people? 1

CHAPLAIN: Yes.

The all important ministry of 'presence'

The minister reported that she did visit her doctor, and that an appointment with a psychiatrist was arranged. So her problem of 'madness' was to go to a higher authority. The likelihood is that answers were no more easily found in that interview, and that she was given more treatment to 'calm her down', possibly as an out-patient, but more likely from her general practitioner. Her fears may have abated by themselves, as she negotiated the particular life issues which she was facing at that time, or they may have grown worse. What she does know now, is that she has a minister who is able and prepared to listen to her. The danger is that he may not appreciate the significance of this for her. He may have thought that her doctor and psychiatrist were better qualified and better placed to help her, and so have undervalued the importance of his continuing ministry. More than anything else Pam needs his belief in her capacity to work this out, or at least to bear the burden of not working it out, with dignity and self respect.

Joan

Beginning

Beginning a relationship is never easy; like the putting together of different and separate objects, we experience a clumsiness and mismatching, a self-consciousness and embarrassment. We often exchange names with each other only to find minutes later that we have not really taken them in. And yet beginnings are important, they reveal our freshness and vulnerability, which soon become hidden again in our conventional ways of relating.

1 Joan takes the initiative in this beginning, by recognizing and then clarifying that her visitor is the Anglican chaplain. In doing so she touches a sensitive area for the chaplain, who is new to both chaplaincy and

JOAN: But where do you work? 2

CHAPLAIN *(evasively):* I'm just learning.

JOAN: But what church do you work for?

CHAPLAIN: Anglican. 3

JOAN: Oh yes. I'm a Roman Catholic. But I have nothing against Anglicans, and the Anglican vicar comes to see my husband. He's an Anglican. But I've lost my faith anyway. And my life is over now. I have nothing left. 4

(At this point the chaplain notices another member of staff washing up on her own, and feels she ought to go and help. She rejoins Joan when she has finished.)

CHAPLAIN: I'm sorry I broke off the conversation back there. I felt I should help with the washing-up. 5

JOAN: No — I didn't feel you'd broken off. I knew you had to help with the washing up.

CHAPLAIN: You were saying to me that you'd lost your faith. How long ago was that?

2 Anglicanism. The chaplain, however, was more confident about her position as a learner, as someone who, by definition, did not yet know what and how she ought to be, but was endeavouring to learn by doing.

3 Joan, sensing where there is a 'fit' in this relationship, explains that though of a different denomination, she has something in common with the chaplain, namely the
4 Anglican vicar who comes to see her husband. But the fit goes no further than that, for she remembers that she has lost her faith. 'My life is over . . . I have nothing left.' Such a challenge is enough to make this chaplain retreat to the 'duty' of the washing-up.

It is no surprise to find that beginnings are a matter of trial and error, of sparring and testing, of coming close and drawing back. The importance of enduring this difficult part of relationships cannot be over emphasized. For in recognizing that beginnings are not easy, we can also notice that the nature of their uneasiness is often a foretaste of the work that is to follow.

5 *A second beginning*

It may not seem all that courageous of the chaplain to return to the scene of her flight but I am sure it was, and it will be courage that we most often need to prevent us from running off literally or metaphorically. Joan, of course, is not surprised that her 'problem' should frighten the chaplain.

JOAN: Oh years! Oh, I used to say my prayers but it was just saying words. There was no feeling in it. Anyway you don't have to talk to me. You can't help me. No one can. 6

CHAPLAIN: Did you lose your faith because you had a stroke?

JOAN: Oh no! The stroke is just bad luck. I don't feel I'm being punished or anything like that. I just don't believe there is a God. And I don't want to live any more. I wish I could die. I'd like to commit suicide, but I'm disabled and I can't even go out and buy a bottle of aspirin. 7

CHAPLAIN: Don't you think your family would be upset if you did that? 8

JOAN: Oh, yes, they would. But I feel I'm a burden to them and to my husband.

CHAPLAIN: Does your husband feel that way? I'm sure he doesn't.

JOAN: I don't know. But I feel it. Anyway I can't talk any more. It makes me tired. 9

(Joan returns to her book. The chaplain picks up a magazine. After a while Joan speaks again.)

6 it has been frightening her for a long time, so long that she has exhausted all the obvious remedies, explanations and avoidances, and wishes only to stop being a burden to herself and others.

7 Perhaps she finds some fatalistic relief in deciding that no one can help, even if that includes the disability which prevents her helping herself to death.

8 Faced with this level of despair the chaplain casts about for some hitherto unnoticed or untried avenue of hope. Perhaps she matters to her family. No! She is just a burden to them, and she is very tired of hunting for hope.

9 The chaplain could have said: 'You sound very sure and very resigned . . .' So for a second time the courage of the chaplain is tested. Can she tolerate such hopelessness? Will she take the dismissal at face value and leave a tired and desperate person to her sufferings? We know about the elderly and eccentric, whose continued rejections of our attempts to help are but a test of our capacity and trustworthiness. It is easier to understand the rejections and dismissals with hindsight; at the time we feel rejected and dismissed. Those we would like to help give us a graphic and frightening sense of what it is like to be them at this moment, rejected and dismissed by themselves. 'I don't want to live anymore, I wish I could die.' On this occasion the chaplain sat out Joan's dismissal of her and, what is more, resisted saying anything else.

JOAN: The thing is it's been going on for so long. And I've asked for help, but help doesn't come. 10

(The chaplain then asks about her illness, and Joan tells her the story of fifteen years of illness following the death of her father to whom she was tied by 'love and hate'. She has been treated with psychotherapy and has made a good recovery. She had taken a degree in sociology and also worked for a charity. The chaplain listens to her story, encouraging her to tell it in her own way and intervening as little as possible. Joan ends it in the following way.)

JOAN: It's very nice of you to be so patient with me. 11

CHAPLAIN: 'Not at all. You're a very interesting person to talk to.

10 Often we feel bound to speak in order to help, and particularly at those times, when we are least sure of what to say. We find it hard to wait and listen, and to let our words be informed less by our own anxieties, and more by 'being with' the one we are trying to help.

Being with

We are inclined to think of help as an answer to prayer, an explanation, a way of seeing things, a tangible change. We visualize it intellectually and verbally, And yet, recalling our experiences of being helped, often it is not so much what others say but what they were and did which made the difference. Sitting with Joan, the chaplain helps by simply being there. That such a truth is a surprise to us as pastors, is an indication of how the intellectualizing of our faith has stolen so much of its potency from us. The notion of God being 'with us' implicit in the Old Testament, and explicit in the New, is the surest foundation for all pastoral work. The parable of the sheep and the goats dramatizes so graphically the fact that we cannot begin unless we are with, really and truly with, ourselves and one another and so with God.[8]

11 The conversation changes at this point, the challenge and testing is over, the mutual exploration and encouragement has begun. The chaplain's position, as a fellow-traveller through life's complexities, enables her to be with Joan as an interested and concerned companion. Elsewhere in this book reference is made to the important qualities which the inexperienced, as opposed to the experienced, helper can bring to the work of helping.[9] Here is a good example of just that.

JOAN: Yes, but I'm not a very nice person since they took me off the drugs. I think I was a more cheerful person before. 12

CHAPLAIN: Why are you off the drugs?

JOAN: Because the doctors say they are harmful. I don't know. I suppose they're right. I'd just like to die. 13

CHAPLAIN: How do you feel about death? Does it frighten you?

JOAN: Oh no! If there isn't a God, then I'll just be finished. It will all be over. If there is a God, then he'll understand. He'll just carry me away in his arms. He won't send me to hell. *(A pause.)* . . . Do you believe in God? 14

CHAPLAIN: Yes, I do.

JOAN: That's good. That's a comfort to me. Even if I can't believe in God, it's a comfort to know that other people can. 15

CHAPLAIN: It seems to me that you would like to believe in God.

Getting lost

Joan has told her story and has heard the chaplain's 12 affirmation of it and of her. Strengthened by that she returns to her present predicament. She does not like herself, and the medication that once obscured her nastiness has been taken away. Ironically the chaplain, rather than exploring her feelings, takes refuge in questions about drugs, as if to help her hide again.

13 Joan is not so easily deterred, the way out of her predicament is death. The chaplain's first question is all she needed to ask. How does Joan feel about death?

14 Joan puts an end to all this nonsense, the problem is not death or dying but living, and the sooner they get back to that the better.

15 She is no longer concerned with the chaplain's ability to help her, she knows instinctively that she has a valuable ally, but one whose skills as a helper require harnessing. For a moment the chaplain pauses and encourages Joan to lead the way. 'It seems to me that you would like to believe in God.'

JOAN: Yes, but I can't. 16

CHAPLAIN: Have you tried talking to him? It's like a relationship with a person. If you don't ever talk to me, how can you get to know me?

JOAN: Oh yes, I know. I can talk to you, but how can I talk to someone when I have no evidence that he's there?

(The chaplain tries two more arguments for belief in God, which Joan rejects. There is a pause, during which the chaplain recalls praying for help.)

JOAN: Will you pray for me? 17

CHAPLAIN: Certainly.

JOAN: Thank you, that's comforting. It's very good of you to be so kind.

CHAPLAIN: Not at all. That's the least we can do for each other.

JOAN: No, no. Any human kindness is good, but kindness based on religious belief is better.

CHAPLAIN: Why?

JOAN: I don't know.

CHAPLAIN *(trying to get back to the basis for the loss of faith):* Can you tell me how it was that you lost your faith and stopped going to church? 18

16 When Joan replies that she 'can't', the chaplain is away again, breaking the harness in a frantic attempt to find an argument that will persuade Joan that she should. There is a proper place to discuss the reasons for believing in God, but the desperate are rarely, if ever, comforted or convinced by arguments.

17 Joan cannot make much use of the chaplain's explanations, but the knowledge that the chaplain will and does pray for Joan is worth something.

Found again

18 The chaplain, in some desperation, returns to the point where her own enthusiasm led her away from Joan. How Joan lost her faith is more to the point than premature attempts to make her regain it. And how she lost it reveals a bit more of Joan's story.

JOAN: I don't think I ever prayed properly. But I think what really made me angry was when I heard on the radio about those Irish priests hiding arms for the IRA. There were a lot of Irish in the church where we lived. And Irish priests. I couldn't bear it. 19

(The chaplain recalls her feeling of panic at this point. Their conversation was interrupted by another visitor, to the relief of the chaplain. Later, after the visitor had left, she thanks Joan for talking with her.) 20

CHAPLAIN: Well, you have been very helpful to me. 21

JOAN *(interested for a change):* Really, how?

CHAPLAIN: Well, I am trying to learn how best to bring help to people in hospitals, apart from the help you're already getting from the staff here. Now, you started a conversation with me about God and faith, and that

19 Her guess that she may never have prayed properly speaks of a sense of not being 'proper' or 'right' – just as priests who store guns affront some basic ethic. The chaplain wants to reduce the power of this revelation, but Joan knows that it cannot be explained away, that was when she stopped wanting to go to Church.

20 The chaplain admits she felt out of her depth, and so much so that she was unable to grasp how important and accurate her feeling was. For she and Joan had become very close together at that moment, confronting questions to which there are no easy answers. At such times we probably say more for God by speaking less, but it does not feel like that. We feel compelled to stand up for him and to save his good name. St Teresa's famous protest to God about her sufferings, 'when you treat them this badly, no wonder you have so few friends', is reminiscent of many of the psalms in which the worshippers were clearly uninhibited in blaming God for their frustration, anger and dereliction. 'My God, my God, why have you forsaken me?' is no theological defence of a God out there, and on the lips of Jesus proclaims a more complex theological truth of a God literally in the midst of the pain of unanswered questions.

21 *Ending*

If 'genuineness' is one of the essential characteristics of an effective helper,[10] then this exchange speaks very well for the chaplain. She shares with Joan the value that this conversation has been to her, that she is trying to learn what it is that God has to offer us in our distress and our need. The chaplain has begun to learn, as perhaps Job's comforters did, the inadequacy of some of the things she has tried to say. There is a hint that she still feels that gave me a chance to talk to you about these matters, and to think hard how to answer the questions raised, how to help you, if possible. I don't think I've done very well, but still, I appreciate the chance you have given me to talk to you.

JOAN: Oh, but you have helped me. You have brought me *your* faith, and I can rest on that, even if I have none of my own. 22

CHAPLAIN: It's very kind of you to say that.

JOAN *(whose most pressing problem is insomnia):* When you wake in the middle of the night, will you think of me and say a prayer for me? 23

CHAPLAIN: I certainly shall. I've prayed for you every day since we met. But do you think my prayers can help, if yours can't? How?

JOAN: I don't know, but perhaps they can.

improved explanations will help Joan most, but Joan makes clear what is the real basis of good pastoring.

22 'You have helped me because you brought me your faith.' The chaplain has demonstrated this by what she has been and what she has done, more than by anything she has said. By being there in the first place, by weathering Joan's dismissal and her own sense of panic, and by genuinely affirming what Joan has done for her, the chaplain has conveyed more than words could express. Joan cannot say how this has helped and yet she knows it has. Many of the chaplain's responses reveal how inexperienced a counsellor she is. She ignored Joan's most significant feelings, pursued the content rather than the emotional weight of what Joan said, and she tried to divert rather than to follow Joan's own explorations. But what she has offered does compensate for her lack of expertise, which practice and experience will improve. The chaplain knows she is a learner and that her faith and her hope are based, not upon where she is at the moment, but on an honest recognition of where she is and whither she is moving. The chaplain symbolizes the movement, not of flight from painful and difficult reality, but of the first attempts to enter into that reality and to learn what it means.

23 And Joan has found a companion for her journey, if she can find the strength to make it.

Emma

Emma is a woman in her thirties in a psychiatric hospital because of deep depression, the cause of which no one can identify. The following is the chaplain's record of a conversation he had with her, when he noticed how distressed she was.

CHAPLAIN: Have you had a bad day? 1

EMMA: Yes, rotten. I can't pull myself together. I have been here for seven weeks and I don't get any better. I went to occupational therapy but I simply froze and cried and cried.

CHAPLAIN: You are very upset, aren't you? 2

EMMA *(breaking down):* Everything collapsed when my father went.

CHAPLAIN: He left home?

EMMA: No, no, not that.

CHAPLAIN: I am sorry. You must have been very close to your father.

EMMA: It was five years ago. I ought to be able to pull myself together. Other people do.

CHAPLAIN: It takes a long time to get over a bereavement. 3

EMMA: I don't want to go on. I am such an evil person. I have tried to make my mother hate me so I would have an excuse to do what I wanted to do. She is a wonderful person. I don't deserve a mother like that, but she still keeps on loving me. Sometimes I think the devil is in me. I used to go to church, but when my father died I couldn't understand why God had taken him. I prayed so hard for him to stay with us. I couldn't hold on to my faith.

Emma

Permission to feel bad

1 In the conversation Emma expresses the agony of her grief about her father; like a bubbling volcano it erupts even when she tries to get on with her ordinary daily affairs. 'I went to occupational therapy, but I simply froze' (holding down), and 'cried and cried' (letting out).

2&3 The pastor gives her permission to be unhappy, pointing out the appropriateness of such feelings. 'It takes a long time to get over bereavement.' Helped by this, Emma begins to say how bad, how ungrateful and how potentially destructive she is. For her, such things can only be explained by some external agency, the devil. She has lost her faith, for God took away her father.

CHAPLAIN: You can't hold on to God but God can hold on to you. You seem to be weighed down with guilt. Do you have any guilt about your father's death? 4

EMMA: Towards the end I felt I could have done more for him.

CHAPLAIN: What in particular?

EMMA: I don't really want to tell you.

CHAPLAIN: Do try. 5

EMMA: Well, on the Sunday before he died my mother had gone to work, and he felt very cold and poorly. *(At this point she breaks down and buries her head in her hands.)* I can't talk about it. I wouldn't allow myself to help him.

4 The chaplain responds partially to her feelings, 'Do you have any guilt?', but also reassures himself as well as her by claiming that God really can hold on to all of this.

5 Emma is not sure, and when the chaplain tries to talk about her guilt, in his eagerness he presses too hard. It would have been more helpful if he had recognized the difficulty she was having. For instance he could have said, 'Emma, it is difficult for you to talk about this, but I also feel you want to try to'.

Excavating for meaning

The metaphor of digging is illuminating here. Emma is scrabbling down to uncover things which hurt her, and which she has tried so hard to keep buried. As she digs, it all becomes too much for her, she cannot speak, because she has never told anyone before. The chaplain, watching from a distance, encourages her to keep going. What he fails to do is to get down with her, to add his weight to her digging and to feel for himself something of the fear and panic which hinder her. There are many reasons why we find entering into another person's distress difficult. Will we too be buried? Will we push the other person too far? Is it a case of the blind leading the blind? And yet these questions may well be the same questions with which people like Emma are struggling. Will I be overwhelmed? Is there any understanding to be got out of this? Will I bury both of us and so destroy the person who is good enough to try and help me?

CHAPLAIN: I think it would help if you could. 6

EMMA: I can't, I have never told anyone.

CHAPLAIN: Whenever anyone dies, it is natural for us to feel guilty. *(The chaplain then tells her a story from his own experience of bereavement.)* 7

EMMA: I know I'm being punished because I didn't help him when he needed help.

CHAPLAIN: Do you think you could possibly write it down? 8

EMMA: (Silence.)

CHAPLAIN: Who do you think is punishing you?

EMMA: God is punishing me because I am so wicked.

6 So the chaplain might have drawn upon his own feelings as a possible guide to Emma's and said: 'I can sense how much it hurts to remember that something actually stopped you helping him. What was that?' For this takes the chaplain down into Emma's distress; he, so to speak, puts his hand over hers to give weight to her excavations. And when she still cannot go on, she needs the pastor to notice and accept that as well. 'And something stops you now, as though you are not allowed to speak about it, even to help yourself.'

When the going is too difficult

The rest of the conversation demonstrates how Emma and her chaplain are left suspended; the unmentionable has been mentioned, but cannot be engaged with further.

7 The chaplain climbs up to a safer position by beginning to generalize about bereavement and guilt.

8 He suggests that she put her horror on paper, where it will be safer to handle. Emma joins him by providing the theological carrot of a God who punishes, to which he responds with a God who forgives.

CHAPLAIN: God is like Jesus. He understands why you acted as you did. He doesn't punish anyone. 9

EMMA: I desperately need help. I get such terrible dreams. I see my father in such awful ways, as when he died clinging to me.

CHAPLAIN: What kind of man was your father?

EMMA: He was such a good man. He didn't deserve a wicked daughter. I deserve to be punished.

CHAPLAIN: Do you believe in forgiveness? Do you believe your father has forgiven you?

EMMA (*grudgingly*): Yes.

CHAPLAIN: Do you believe God has forgiven you? God can't be less loving than your father.

9 The chaplain tries to reason her out of her distress, but is left with little doubt about the guilt which envelops Emma. Both of them are left wondering whether she can allow herself to get better.

Their conversation is a vivid example of the possibilities and the problems of the pastoral relationship. The chaplain, by his manner and sensitive concern, provides sufficient security and trust for Emma to begin to search for what is troubling her. His attentiveness and willingness to listen, and not to judge her, makes it possible for her to say what she has never said before. He offers her his attention, empathy and respect,[11] until the weight of what is being uncovered is too much for both of them. What is difficult for them to acknowledge is the appropriateness of their fear, and that they need to draw breath psychologically before going further.

Mistakes that reveal the meaning

Of course it is easier with hindsight to see where the interview failed for lack of nerve or of patience on the part of the helper and helped. On the surface such hindsight can be very intimidating to the helper, who, in this case, was convinced he had failed Emma. But, in another way, getting it 'wrong' and seeing how and where that has happened is as valuable as getting it 'right'. The point at which Emma and her chaplain retreated from pain and the way in which they did it, provide vital clues as to the nature of what is happening to Emma. She would not allow herself to help her father,
8 and she would not allow herself to talk. In both cases she failed because of her will-power, and so in her mind
9 she deserves to be punished. This in turn provokes the chaplain to his sermon on forgiveness, as though he too thinks she is wrong, this time for misunderstanding the nature of God.

10

EMMA: I ought to be punished. I am being punished. If it wasn't for my mother I would end it all, but I know I would take her with me. I would like to die and be with my father, but I know I couldn't be, because I would be in hell. I believe in hell. I live in hell.

CHAPLAIN: Emma, you seem to be enveloped in a terrible black cloud of guilt. Do you want to get better?

EMMA: I have been asked that question before. I want to be free of this thing which is totally destroying me. I am so wicked, I know I deserve to be punished.

10 He pushes her to change her mind, and once again her stubbornness is reinforced: 'I'm wicked, I deserve the punishment.' The mistakes and diversions of pastoral counselling are the vital raw material of helping, paradoxically more so than the successes. For they have written within them an uncanny reflection of the mistakes and difficulties of the person seeking help, who is, after all, concerned more with the effect of her failures than she is with her success.

Bearing one another's burdens

This is a good example of the way in which a pastor can shoulder some of the distress of the pastored. The chaplain in this case came away bearing a sense of failure, for which he got support in supervision. Later he heard how relieved Emma was as a result of their talk, and that she now felt the Church to be more approachable and helpful.

Ray

Ray is forty and married with three children. He has served a long-term prison sentence and is now in hospital for assessment and rehabilitation. It is unlikely that he will return to live with his family in the short term, and at present his social worker is trying to help him find alternative accommodation. The chaplain has spoken to him on a number of occasions, and has noted how upset he is by other people's anger. By talking to him further he hopes to try and understand why this is so. In this conversation they were sitting together in the lounge on the ward where Ray is a patient.

RAY: Will I ever get better? 1

CHAPLAIN: That's a great dread for you?

RAY: Yes, I've been feeling so uptight over the past week. Little things get you down. Some people get it out of their system by making a lot of noise. All the noise gets me down. *(Here he puts his hands over his forehead.)* It's like being back in prison. People crashing about and shouting and fighting.

CHAPLAIN: What does that make you feel?

RAY: I've had enough of it. I was nine years in prison. 2 And now I am trying to make a new start. They let me go on a couple of mornings to see the children.

CHAPLAIN: How old are the children?

RAY: Ten. They're twins. And there's another one, but he's at work. I am not so worried about him.

CHAPLAIN: You don't feel so easy about the other two? 3

Ray

Finding the feelings beneath the facts

1 Ray voices the question which gnaws away at the confidence of most, if not every patient: 'Will I ever get better?', and the chaplain helps him bring it from the general to the specific,[12] from 'we' to 'me'.

2 Ray explains his feelings, and then, perhaps to relieve himself of them, thinks of his children. Being a father is better than being a prisoner or a patient.

3 The chaplain notes his concern about the younger ones and so helps him voice his fears.

RAY: I had last Christmas with them. The first I had for years. And just to think I won't be with them next Christmas.

CHAPLAIN: Why is that? 4

RAY: Well, marriage breakdown, isn't it. 5

CHAPLAIN: This is something that has happened recently?

RAY: About two months ago.

CHAPLAIN: What is the present position?

RAY: Well, she still comes to see me. And I respect her. She is a lovely woman. She has been a good wife and mother. I still love her. The only thing is that she feels more secure without me now than with me. 6

(There is an interruption.)

RAY: I get to see the children as much as I can. I only hope they don't get a court order against me restricting my visits.

CHAPLAIN: Who are 'they'? 7

RAY: My wife, and my wife's mother, and my brother-in-law. They would put me in a doss-house. You see, my wife's mother lives with her. And all the decisions get made between the two of them. I know the children are enjoying themselves. I couldn't stand being left out. Still, the hospital is trying to find me a flat.

Ray is no longer able to be a proper father, and this Christmas will bring confirmation of the fact.

4 At this point the chaplain is preoccupied with the facts when Ray is trying to express his feelings.

5 He has to pull the chaplain along. 'Well, marriage breakdown, isn't it.' It would have been better had the chaplain contained his curiosity and just followed Ray's exploration, at (4) he could have said: 'What is it like to think about not being with them next Christmas?'

The hurt of exclusion

6 Ray explains the present position and lets drop the fact that he is now excluded from both being a parent and being a husband. His wife feels more secure without him. If there had not been an interruption at this point, the chaplain could have asked him how that felt for him. 'She feels more secure without you, how is it for you . . . loving her as you do?'

When Ray goes on to talk about the children and his fears of being completely excluded from seeing them, the chaplain again responds to the facts rather than Ray's feelings about the facts.

7 A better response would have been: 'You fear they might do that and wonder how you will cope if they do.' Nevertheless Ray goes on to reveal the basis of some of his feelings about his wife's family, and how much it will hurt him to be left out of the children's enjoyment.

CHAPLAIN: And you will move into that as soon as they find one? 8

RAY: Yes, if I am well enough that is.

CHAPLAIN: What is the future going to be for you?

RAY: It's going to be difficult to get a job. I've been to the town hall. I realized it would be difficult to get employment so I have been asking if there is some voluntary work that I can do. But nobody wants you. I went to the social services and I went to the churches, Roman Catholic, Church of England, the Salvation Army said they might have something. *(He then speaks of how he feels the church has let him down, had not helped him when he came out of prison and had often rejected his offers of help. It was 'dogma' that kept getting in the way.)* 9

CHAPLAIN: I suppose the hard reality is that churches don't always accept people straight away. Perhaps you have to be around for a bit, and then gradually . . . 10

RAY *(angrily):* Look, brother, Jesus accepted people immediately, and taught his disciples to do that. He didn't say that they should accept people gradually.

CHAPLAIN: That is an important thing for me to think about. But what about you? 11

RAY: It's not just me. It's thousands of people.

8 Yet again the chaplain conveys his own difficulty with Ray's distress, by ignoring it and taking up the practical issue of a flat and then the future in general.

9 Ray, however, weaves his distress back into the conversation. He knows that it would be difficult to get work at present, but he had not imagined that voluntary work would be equally difficult to find. It appears that like his family, no one wants him, not even the churches!

10 *What can be done with anger*

The chaplain's response is certainly realistic, but it shows no recognition of Ray's distress now turned to anger, and because of this Ray makes his feelings clear.

11 The chaplain acknowledges the rebuke, but again misses the opportunity to help Ray with his anger, and the hurt that lies beneath it. He could have done this by showing the link between Ray's feelings of rejection by his family and by the churches: 'I think I can begin to understand why you are so angry. Your family have rejected you and you fear they will go on doing that. And the churches, who are supposed to be accepting, are rejecting you as well. It's like being kicked again when you are down. It hurts more than you can stand.' By such a response the chaplain would convey his readiness to be with Ray 'out in the cold'.

CHAPLAIN: O.K. But I am thinking about you right now. I am concerned that you should not be out in the cold.' 12

(Ray then speaks about his faith in Christ and Christ's power to heal.)

CHAPLAIN: At the beginning of our talk you were asking whether you would ever get better. How do you feel in the light of what you have just been saying? 13

RAY: Christ does not always heal people. So far as I am concerned it is his will that matters.

CHAPLAIN: Do you blame yourself at all?

RAY: Oh no, it is a matter of his will. And it hasn't lessened my faith at all. *(He then speaks about the church and its need of faith. He mentions, however, that he does know clergy and ministers who are doing a good job.)* 14

CHAPLAIN: So you are in touch with some people who are doing the work in what you feel is the right way. 15

RAY: Yes.

12 Instead he expresses his wish to bring Ray 'in from the cold'. At one level there may not seem to be a great difference, and yet the former has a basis in reality, difficult as that reality is, which the latter ignores. All the wishing in the world will not bring Ray in from the cold, understanding why he is there is more likely to succeed, particularly if he is not alone in his exclusion.

Moving to safer ground

13 In the remainder of their conversation, Ray and the chaplain appear to be searching for an explanation of their relative positions. Separated by Ray's anger and sense of exclusion, they turn away from the rawness of the feelings they have encountered.

14 Religion, in a more general sense, is used as a balm to soothe the hurt. Christ can heal, but he doesn't always do it; his will is what matters.

15 There is too a relief in Ray's acknowledgement that some clergy get it right.

Conversations which touch upon important and powerful feelings do need to find their way back to less stressful things before they end. And this conversation is an example of how that was achieved. The pity is that it is achieved with pastor and pastored separated, and so mirroring the rejection and exclusion which are at the heart of Ray's situation. If the chaplain could have allowed himself to be the object of Ray's anger, the representative of the uncaring church, he would have helped Ray discover more of the meaning of that anger, and of its contribution to his predicament. The chaplain would have been a living embodiment of a 'church' which accepted Ray, anger and all.

Edward

Edward is in his late twenties, a patient in a psychiatric hospital, recently admitted because he was knocked down by a bus, when he may have been trying to kill himself. The chaplain at the hospital to which he was first taken because of his injuries, referred him to the chaplain at the psychiatric hospital, who calls to see him. He finds Edward lying on his bed, looking very shaken.

CHAPLAIN: Hello, you are Edward. I'm the hospital chaplain. 1

EDWARD: Hello.

CHAPLAIN: The chaplain at the other hospital you went to, told me you were here and suggested that I come to see you.

(Edward sits on the bed and the chaplain on a chair. Edward looks very confused.)

CHAPLAIN: You look rather overwhelmed! You've been having a difficult time?

EDWARD *(nodding agreement):* I don't know what has happened to me. *(He struggles to pull himself together.)* I don't know . . . I don't seem to be real anymore. *(He checks his hands to see if they are his, and then winces as if his back hurts.)* 2

CHAPLAIN: Would it help to lie down while we talk?

EDWARD: I don't know . . . no, I think I will stand. *(He looks at himself in the mirror, looking for something, and then at the chaplain.)* I don't know what has happened, I was going in one direction and everything was all right, and then it all changed . . . *(pause).*

Edward

Losing touch with reality

1 The chaplain finds Edward agitated and confused. He quietly explains why he has come, and then responds to Edward's distress.

2 This allows Edward to explain something of the fear that lies behind his agitation. He no longer feels real and when he looks at himself in the mirror, his doubts are confirmed, there has been a dramatic change in his life.

CHAPLAIN: Like the parting of the ways, you were on a different road, and one it is hard even to describe. 3

EDWARD: I was all right. I was good, other people told me I wasn't, but I know I was . . . It must be a punishment . . . *(pause).*

CHAPLAIN: A punishment? 4

EDWARD: Yes. *(Suddenly alert and frightened.)* You think that I'm being punished?

CHAPLAIN: No! I was trying to understand how you experienced it. That somehow you felt you were all right, and others didn't. Then this happened and you wondered if they were right after all. 5

EDWARD: Yes, perhaps I was wrong. And that's why I am being punished. The trouble is I don't seem to be real, I'm spiritually dead. *(He looks at his hands and his face again, as though to confirm what he has just said.)*

3 The chaplain responds by reflecting back to Edward what he has said, and also his appreciation of how difficult it is for Edward to find words to describe his experience.

4 When he does find the word 'punishment', the chaplain's echoing of that has a frightening effect. Edward feels that his worst fears are right. This demonstrates the problem of responding effectively to someone who is as confused and ill as Edward is. He has only a tenuous hold on reality and can no longer manage words and ideas reasonably. At times he is oblivious of the chaplain, at other times he latches on to something he says as though he suddenly finds a place for it.

5 *The different worlds of the sane and insane*

The chaplain tries to extricate himself and explains how he has understood Edward's dilemma. But Edward is away again with his own thoughts, fitting the notion of punishment into place. If he was wrong, then it is quite logical to expect punishment.

CHAPLAIN: You look for yourself, but you can't see what you are looking for? 6

EDWARD *(looking very frightened):* I'll go to hell. Do you think I'll go to hell?

CHAPLAIN: No, I don't know that, but I hear you saying that is what you fear. Something terrible has happened to you and you are searching for an explanation equal in proportion. 7

(Edward thinks about this for a while, looking at himself in the mirror again, and then relaxes a little.)

CHAPLAIN: Edward, you said earlier about being good, and now somehow bad, as though you were neither one nor the other. 8

EDWARD *(thinking and then nodding):* Yes.

CHAPLAIN: St Paul once expressed what sounds to me like the same thing. 'Why do we do the evil we don't want, rather than the good that we do want.' For me that says quite a lot about the struggle for good and bad in me. I wonder if it's like that for you at the moment?

(Edward looks puzzled but interested.)

CHAPLAIN: I suppose what is hardest is having to face what seems bad about ourselves. Maybe we run away, or we attack it and try to destroy it. 9

EDWARD: Destroy it? What do you mean?

CHAPLAIN: I'm not sure, but perhaps your walking under a bus was about that?

6 This is a more helpful response by the chaplain. He does not try to fathom the depths of Edward's chaotic mind, he responds to what he sees and feels, and so conveys his readiness to be with Edward. Meanwhile Edward's train of thought has taken him from punishment to hell.

7 The chaplain copes well with this question. First, by his firm denial of Edward's conclusion, and then by his reiteration of the circumstances which have given Edward such terrifying ideas. So the chaplain halts Edward's flight into more and more frightening speculations.

Explanations versus sanctuary

8 Unfortunately, the chaplain does not stop there. He takes advantage of the silence to embark upon his way of explaining Edward's experience. By referring to St Paul he tries to offer Edward some comfort for his condition. If Edward could appreciate that St Paul had similar experiences to his own, then surely that would help. The chaplain's motives are right, his timing inappropriate. He would have been better advised to keep this theological understanding as a comfort for himself, and as a support for his ministry to Edward, and not presume that it could or would help Edward at this point.

9 As is already obvious, Edward's ability to grasp even a simple idea is much impaired. Trying to follow the chaplain's connection between wanting to destroy something bad and his walking under a bus is beyond Edward.

EDWARD: Mm . . . *(He nods.)* Will I ever get out of this? 10

CHAPLAIN: From where you are at the moment, you don't think you will?

EDWARD *(very agitated again):* You don't think I will?

CHAPLAIN: No, I was saying how I thought it was for you. I think it is our job here to help you find a way out. Like you are in a trough, and have to trust us to be up a bit higher and able to see a little further. 11

EDWARD *(more relaxed):* I want . . . I want to get out of this.

CHAPLAIN: And while it's so bad you don't see how . . . *(pause).*

EDWARD: Perhaps it's meant, like God means it.

CHAPLAIN: That's what is so hard to tell. Is it something to do with me, or God, or both? In the garden of Gethsemane Jesus said, 'I don't want this to go on, but if it is what you want, then it must . . .' because it does have some point. 12

EDWARD: If it has some point . . .

CHAPLAIN: That's what's so hard for you at this moment. Like searching for yourself . . . you were doing earlier . . . *(After a pause during which Edward again looks puzzled):* Edward, I am afraid I have to go now, but I would like to come and talk to you again if I may? If it helps we have a service on Sundays, and you are very welcome to come if you want to. 13

EDWARD *(nodding):* . . . Will I get better?

10 It is now Edward's turn to bring the chaplain back to earth by asking whether he, Edward, will ever get out of this. The chaplain reflects the uncertainty Edward feels and again Edward hears that as a confirmation of his fears. He is not in a position at this stage to explore and understand what is happening to him. What he needs most is the security and the sanctuary to await his gradual recovery. He needs the chaplain's presence and reassurance much more than he needs counselling.

11 The chaplain's response, that it is the job of the people here to help him find a way out, is useful to Edward.

12 When however the chaplain goes on to explain the experience Edward is going through, by referring to Jesus in the gardens of Gethsemane, Edward is again puzzled. To hear that the chaplain thinks he will get better, even though it will take time, is more helpful. It gives him hope and encourages his patients.

13 By continuing to call and see him the chaplain will reinforce both.

CHAPLAIN: I think so, but I think it will take time.

EDWARD: . . . time . . .

CHAPLAIN: It's hard to hang on . . .

EDWARD: Yes.

CHAPLAIN *(getting up and taking hold of Edward's hand):* God bless you Edward. I will come and see you again.

EDWARD: Mm . . . *(He sits back on the bed.)*

Sarah

Sarah is twenty-five, and has been in hospital for over a year, following a major breakdown at university. While in hospital, she has appreciated the chaplain's ministry to her. Prior to his visit she had been very ill, and hardly aware of his presence. On this occasion she did greet him and they sat down together.

CHAPLAIN: How have you been, Sarah? 1

SARAH *(pausing):* Better I think . . . I'm on medication now, and that makes me feel better . . . but I'm not really better.

CHAPLAIN: Mm . . . *(pause).*

SARAH: I don't know, I'm not sure anymore . . .

CHAPLAIN: Feeling better doesn't stop you worrying about how you really are?

(Sarah nods, begins to say something and then withdraws into herself. After some time she turns slightly to look at the chaplain, and then hurriedly turns away.)

This is a good example of how unconsciously the patient's distress and anxiety infect the chaplain. Like a physical infection it draws out the chaplain's own resources to fight it. Hence the chaplain's recourse to the theological ideas, which he offers to Edward. Far from having the healing effect he wants, they are at best a barrier between himself and Edward, and, at worst, more poison for Edward's wounds. Because they act like a barrier they are of course an unconscious protection to the chaplain. They get between him and Edward's pain, and that is his unconscious reason for using them. When we find ourselves as pastors breaking into a sermon or a prayer, it is important to ask ourselves for whose benefit we are praying or preaching.

Sarah

The damage I can do

1 Sarah begins coherently enough telling the chaplain that she feels better, but that it is a superficial well-being. Inside, to where she withdraws, it is dark and terrifying.

CHAPLAIN: You look frightened of something? 2

SARAH: I am.

CHAPLAIN: Of what?

SARAH: Of what I've done to you. 3

CHAPLAIN: You've hurt me?

SARAH: No, I've infected you . . . I'm so evil, like a witch.

2 Her look communicates her fear; on many occasions she has spoken of causing harm and unhappiness. Indeed the distress of her family and of the hospital staff confirms her belief that she is bad. 'I'm evil, like a witch.'

3 Now she attributes to herself the death of someone, and her danger to the chaplain. All helpers are faced with a dilemma at this point. Counselling technique suggests that we should follow the feelings of the patient, but as those feelings emerge as delusions, 'it was my fault someone died', it is possible our empathy will reinforce rather than modify those beliefs. On the other hand if we stay firmly with our reality, we run the risk of losing a tenuous hold on someone who is slipping further into madness! It is a narrow line which the helper has to negotiate. Somehow we have to convey two things at once, our understanding of the patient's reality and of our own reality. The former will not be shifted by our reasoning, nor reinforced by our understanding, though it can be by our behaviour. If, for instance, the chaplain were to behave as though Sarah were evil, either by exorcising her evil spirit, or by failing to come and see her, as though being with her were dangerous, then there would be a real risk of confirming her delusions.

CHAPLAIN: And you're frightened that I'm in danger from you? 4

SARAH: Yes . . . someone died . . . and it was my fault.

CHAPLAIN: You believe that you are responsible for someone's death and also for infecting me. That is frightening, and yet so different from how I experience you.

SARAH *(looking puzzled):* What do you mean?

CHAPLAIN: That you do not frighten me. That I want to come and see you however you are. They told Jesus not to go to those who were ill or felt bad and evil, and yet he was happy to go. 5

SARAH *(listening and looking puzzled):* Someone prayed with me the other day . . . but it did not reach . . . 6

CHAPLAIN: It helped a bit but . . .

SARAH: It did not last . . .

CHAPLAIN: Like a medication it did not reach right down to where you feel so bad. 7

(Sarah nods.)

CHAPLAIN: It is hard to grasp, to feel — I don't know which — that there really is nothing that can separate us from the love of God, nothing in heaven or earth . . . I suppose I come and try to represent that, until you can know it for yourself . . . 8
(A long silence.) Shall we pray before I go?

(Sarah nods assent.)

Acknowledging the two realities

4 The chaplain tries to achieve this balance by acknowledging how frightening Sarah's reality is, but also how different it is from his own.

5 He wants to come and see her rather than fears to do so, and suggests that his coming is representative of God being with her.

6 This leads her to recall how God's presence has helped, although it still falls short of what she needs.

7 The chaplain does not contradict her experience but offers her the possibility of leaning on his faith until she can find some of her own.

8 His prayer, his hand on her shoulder and his promise to come again, speak of an acceptance which neither ignores nor judges her 'badness', but awaits its reconciliation with hope.

CHAPLAIN: Lord, your presence matters so much now, like your presence once mattered so much to the hurt and the frightened and especially those who felt beyond contact with you. Be with Sarah, her family and everyone here. *(The chaplain puts his hand on her shoulder.)*

SARAH *(very quietly):* Thank you.

Pastoring the psychotic patient

An explicitly religious response is offered by the two chaplains to Edward and Sarah in apparently similar ways. The difference is in the knowledge they each had of their respective patients. Edward and his religious world are foreign to the first chaplain, and his efforts miss their mark as a result. Sarah's chaplain has spent many hours with her, and at times when she has revealed a great deal about her beliefs, he draws upon that knowledge to good effect. Sarah is still not well, but is now able to bring herself to the hospital chapel and to receive communion, something that was impossible for the 'evil' Sarah, of this conversation, to contemplate doing. The aim of counselling for a patient at this point in their illness is best conveyed by the concept of sanctuary. The chaplain tries to create a relationship in which that, above all, prevails. He is willing and able to be present, to listen to what patients have to say, or more often to sit with them in silence. Not to search for meanings or offer explanations, but rather to wait with patience for the illness to respond to treatment or to run its natural course. While it does, the chaplain needs to make a mental note of what the patient says and how the relationship feels. Strange and incoherent as these things often are, they can come, in time, to make a lot of sense to both pastor and the pastored.

Notes

1. *The Constitutional Papers of the Association for Pastoral Care and Counselling* (1973) has a full definition.
2. See Chapter 6.
3. See Chapter 6, pp. 120–1: Supervision.
4. See Chapter 7, p. 137: Neuroses.
5. As above, p. 138: Psychosis.
6. As above, p. 138: Personality disorders.
7. See Chapter 6, pp. 110–11: Empathy.
8. Matthew 25. 31–46.
9. See Chapter 6, p. 116.
10. See Chapter 6, pp. 115–16: Genuineness.
11. See Chapter 6, pp. 112–13: Respect.
12. See Chapter 6, pp. 113–15: Concreteness.

Further reading

Goffman, E., *Stigma.* Penguin 1968.
Grainger, R. A., *Place Like This.* Regency 1983.
Kesey, K., *One Flew Over the Cuckoo's Nest.* Pan 1973.
Marteau, L., *Words of Counsel.* Shand 1978.

THREE

Counselling with Groups and Institutions

For where two or three are gathered in my name, there am I in the midst of them.[1]

In the examples already recorded, the emphasis has been on pastoral counselling as it manifests itself in the relationship between individuals and their pastors. This has been a deliberate attempt to concentrate on the minutiae of such relationships in order to see what helps and what hinders, how mistakes are redeemed and meaning uncovered. That does not mean that pastoral counselling is only a matter of skill and technique, or only an activity restricted to two people. Indeed, later on it is argued that such an understanding has deprived us of much that is most valuable in the long tradition of pastoral care.[2] All those who have contributed to this book by way of the examples above, were 'pastored' and 'pastoring' with many people in many places. As Mary (in Chapter 4) makes clear, the sub-culture of her ward was rife with the pastoral and spiritual yearnings of its inhabitants.[3] Christian missionary zeal, often masking considerable vocational insecurity, may feed the erroneous belief that it is the Christian who alone brings Christ and is alone responsible for what ever pastoring needs to be done. Those who seek to learn about pastoral counselling in psychiatric hospitals are often amazed and humbled by the pastoral care they receive from the very patients for whom they expected to care.

The examples which follow demonstrate in contrasting ways the nature of pastoral counselling, not as a technique whereby one person helps another, but as a perspective on the working out of salvation – as a way both of observing and contributing to the coming of the Kingdom of God. The first is an explicit example of pastoral counselling within the body of Christ, in a group gathered together specifically to help one another. The second, and more implicit, is the story of how one patient came to be the centre of the co-operative care of his church and family, the hospital and its chaplains.

Faith and Doubt

The group is called 'Faith and Doubt'. It is open to anyone who wants to come, to talk or just to listen. Meeting regularly each week for over four years, membership has varied enormously. Patients have come and gone and returned. Usually there are between six and ten present; Christians and Jews, atheists and agnostics and at least one Moslem, have talked and discussed, prayed and read the Bible, laughed and cried together. The group's only guide is to respond to the issues of 'faith' and 'doubt' as they are expressed by those present on that day. The previous week the group had been preoccupied by the problems of being a 'patient'; of staff being either too human and sharing their feelings, or too professional and distant. There was a sense of anger and resentment at being ill and not getting better. The chaplain began by passing on a message to one of the group, Clive.

CHAPLAIN: Peter told me, Clive, that you had been having a difficult time and might like the chance to talk about it today.

CLIVE (*looking surprised but pleased to be thought about*): Yes, things are bad . . . I'm not sure that talking helps very much. (*With a stifled laugh*) I think I'm having an identity crisis.

GILL: What is an identity crisis?

CLIVE: It is difficult to explain, so many things have been happening. I suppose I am trying to work out who I am, but I can't. Because, well – all the practical details – I could be homeless any time.

ANGELA: What do you mean – homeless?

(*Clive explains about his housing problem.*)

FRANK: You know, Clive, if I was without a home, I would go

and camp on the doorstep of the housing department. They would have to house me.

CLIVE (*laughing*): Oh that's good; I didn't know I could do that. (*Pause.*) I still hope that the move I planned ages back is going to come off. I feel that in a new place I could actually try to be the person I want to be, and not the one everyone expects me to be. What I fear, of course, is that there isn't any me to find.

CHAPLAIN: I remember that feeling when I came to this job. It was good not being a vicar any more, but terrifying when I didn't know how to be me, as a chaplain. I kept going back to friends to check up who I was.

CLIVE: I don't think I can go back, but I don't think I can go on either.

CHAPLAIN: It sounds like you need sanctuary – like the monasteries once were, and now it's hospitals and prisons that provide it. A space where we can just try to be ourselves.

HEATHER: Or a doss-house.

ANGELA: What do you mean – a doss-house?

HEATHER: Well, they are places where you have your bed, and eighteen inches of floor, and no room for possessions and things, and no responsibilities. You can really be yourself. For me it was getting rid of my husband and my middle-class expectations of myself, and actually trying to be me and not what others wanted me to be.

ANGELA: I can understand what Clive is saying, because I feel like that too. I need to be born over again to start from the beginning and make a better job of it.

VALERIE: Yes, you know what you have to do, Clive. Take Jesus for your saviour.

CLIVE: Oh, I wish I could, I wish I had your faith (*said warmly and compassionately*).

CHAPLAIN: Does what Angela said make any sense, Clive?

CLIVE: Yes, it does.

ANGELA: I just have this feeling that I wish I could start again, but I don't see how anyone can.

CHAPLAIN: Like Nicodemus saying to Jesus, 'How can I enter my mother's womb and be born again?'[4] Was your time in the doss-house like that, Heather?

HEATHER: No, not a new birth, more a getting back to what or who I really am. A stripping off of what others have put on me.

RICHARD: There are times when you need to look back, to see how things have gone wrong, and the mistakes you've made. To say sorry for them.

CLIVE: But when I see my mistakes, I think to myself perhaps I wouldn't do them again, but I'm sure that I would, or some others just like them.

(*A lot of laughter.*)

CHAPLAIN: Jane, what about you in all of this? I imagine from what you have said that you have doubts about your start.

JANE: Oh yes, if I were born again the one thing that I would choose would be different parents.

CHAPLAIN: So the feeling of being somehow wrong or a mistake produces a need to search for ourselves, and the realization that it is others who have shaped us. A need to strip all that off. As Clive said to you, Valerie, it's good that you can trust in Jesus, but someone in the 'Nicodemus' position can't just materialize that trust.

CLIVE: You can say that again. It's all very well to say our weaknesses are our strengths, but they don't feel like that.

CHAPLAIN: Hold on though, Clive; haven't you found something very important there? You said earlier that although your mistakes might be different if you had a second chance, they would be similar. Isn't that a clue? Our mistakes really are ours, really are us. Not something that shouldn't be or wouldn't be if we started again.

(*Everyone looks puzzled.*)

Jane do you know what I'm trying to say?

JANE: I'm not sure, but I do know how strong destructive feelings are.

CHAPLAIN: Like what we hate in ourselves we attack. We can sometimes manage compassion for the same things in others, but certainly not in ourselves.

CLIVE: So you mean when we attack our mistakes we're really attacking ourselves.

This example demonstrates the rich repositories of knowledge and understanding, of faith and experience which lie buried in any group of people. Finding the seam, digging for and bringing out the gold is the revelation of pastoral care and the skill of pastoral counselling. The ingredients are all there in a house church, prayer meeting or a group counselling session. Indeed, attending group therapy for the mentally ill at the same time as leading a confirmation class for adults, made me aware of the similarity rather than the difference of these two activities. Each depended for their enrichment upon the individual members who either uncovered within themselves and each other those hidden riches, or else buried them deeper. Of course, the knowledge and training of therapist and pastor, counsellor and catechist, are different, and one might conclude from that, that what they do is different as well. But in fact, the skill of the leader in both instances is that of 'apostle', the one who creates the space in which the 'good news' can be born of the flesh of those who share in its birth. Barth in his commentary on the Epistle to the Romans describes it like this:

> A man may be of value to another man, not because he wishes to be important, not because he possesses some inner wealth of soul, not because of something he is, but because of what he is not. His importance may consist of his poverty, in his hopes and fears, in his waiting and in his hurrying, in the direction of his whole being towards what lies beyond his horizon and beyond his power. The importance of an apostle is negative rather than positive. In him a void becomes visible. And for this reason he is something to others; he is able to share grace with them, to

> focus their attention and to establish them in waiting and in adoration. The spirit gives grace through him.[5]

The chaplain began by making space for Clive, who was not sure how to use the invitation, but was helped by the encouragement of others. They did not turn upon him and try to solve his problems, rather they invited him to share more, and offered their own experience and difficulties to put beside his. The group became a kind of sanctuary, supporting the members to be themselves or, rather, to try to find themselves, relieved of the pressure of being what others wanted them to be. People speculated about the possibility of doing things differently, of a new chance or a fresh start. Such hopes, however, obscure the truth that our mistakes belong to us – in trying to disown or eradicate them, we run the risk of disowning and eradicating ourselves. The 'sinner' is destroyed with the 'sin'. If we succeed in such a conquest we deprive ourselves of that which makes repentance and forgiveness possible.

The example also demonstrates that people hold very different religious world views, and how important it is to recognize this.[6] The chaplain works hard, and we can judge with what effect, to make room for the conflicting views in this group. Some required reference to scripture and the saving knowledge of Christ, while others saw no meaning or significance in anything but the authority of their own experience. The hope would be that each could respect, teach and learn from the other.

Harry

The problems and possibilities of co-operative ministry are well illustrated by the story of Harry. He was a happy and successful family and business man, and a leading member of his local church. Some few years before he was due to retire, he started having problems with his memory. Eventually this became so bad that he agreed to retire early. He was glad to have the chance to spend more time with his grandchildren and with his church activities. Retirement, however, was not as easy as he had expected, his memory continued to let him down, and with more time to himself he worried more about it. He grew morose and withdrawn and, unlike his old self, irritable and unpredictable with his family. At better moments he turned to his church for help, and was comforted by their prayers and support. But when he failed to improve, their unease gathered momentum. Perhaps Harry was possessed; certainly he was now a very different person from the man they had all known and loved. At times Harry was convinced they were right, and was obsessed with his badness. The church prayed for his healing, and on several occasions he had laying on of hands. But this made no difference, and after great heart-searching Harry's wife took him to see a doctor. He was referred to a psychiatrist who immediately admitted him to hospital. There it was shown that he was suffering from senile dementia.[7]

For the next few months Harry was at the centre of an extreme ideological conflict. His church remained convinced that he was not ill, and that he should be got out of the hospital as soon as possible. Some of his family shared that view, and regularly told him to take his discharge. Meanwhile the hospital staff presented the family with the evidence of Harry's brain deterioration, and the need to prepare him and his wife for what was now a terminal illness.

At this point Harry's wife came to the hospital chaplain and shared her distress and confusion. How could she possibly cope with her husband dying slowly and painfully before her eyes, her relatives and friends accusing her of lack of faith, and her own guilt at no longer being able to love Harry in the way she once did. 'Sometimes', she said, 'I don't even want to see him.' At first she and Harry saw the staff as enemies, but gradually their obvious care and concern, together with their respect for Harry's religion, communicated itself. Harry settled into the life of the ward, and his wife was able to talk more freely of her feelings and of the dilemmas she faced, such as her guilt at leaving Harry while she went on holiday. Harry had bad times when he was again overcome by guilt. He lay on his bed moaning and crying, trying to remember some comforting phrases, or he would set off round the ward or out into the hospital to fulfil some task, the nature of which he could not remember. Often it was just one word that he kept repeating, 'Waters . . . waters . . . waters . . .' It was the chaplain who noticed that often such words were from the Bible or a well-known hymn. It was not a drink but 'living waters' that he wanted and was content with, once he had heard the phrase in full. The chaplain gave the ward staff a list of sentences with which to comfort him, and it seemed quite in keeping with their role as nurses to help Harry find the words for his prayers. His friends from the church were much happier too. Freed from the responsibility of making him better, and getting rid of his 'devil', they just came to be with him.

Harry's tragedy had then a hint of triumph. What started in such a divisive and alienating way became the opportunity for co-operation beyond the imagination of any who were involved. Harry is with his family, his own and his adoptive hospital family. His church is all around him now, and when he 'drops' it, there is someone to 'pick' it up for him. What is more, science and religion have come just that little bit closer around his bedside. So, even his illness, unhappy and degrading as it is, has been the occasion of at-one-ment.

The pastoral counsellor brings to these situations a concern for, and interest in, wholeness. Just as the counsellor strives to embrace the whole of a person's experience – feelings and thoughts, the good and the bad – in individual counselling, so here the pastor tries to embrace the whole situation. The splitting and dividing, so destructive within individuals, is often more marked in groups, families and organizations. Good and bad, right and wrong, become the monopoly of particular individuals. For Harry's family the hospital was the last place for him to be. For the hospital it was his church who were destroying him. Pastoral counselling, as a perspective upon and as an agent for, the Kingdom of God, requires us to relate to the bits and pieces only and always as parts of the whole.

Notes

1. Matthew 18.20.
2. See Chapter 8; also A. Campbell, *The Rediscovery of Pastoral Care*, Darton Longman and Todd, 1981.
3. See Chapter 4, pp. 91 and 94.
4. John 3.4.
5. K. Barth, *Epistle to the Romans*, translated by E. Hoskyns, 1933.

6. W. E. Baldridge and J. J. Gleason, 'A Theological Framework for Pastoral Care' (*Journal of Pastoral Care,* XXXII, 4, 1978). The authors elaborate on Tillich's theory of the symbols of faith. They argue that there are three different ways of relating to the symbols of faith, which assume three different spiritual world views. The first is a natural and unconscious literalism. Valerie in the 'Faith and Doubt' group expresses this world view, '. . . What you have to do Clive. Take Jesus for your saviour'. The second is a more conscious or thought-out literalism, which, though acknowledging evidence that conflicts with a simple and literal point of view, nevertheless seeks out more authoritative support for that literal truth. Harry's family and church held on to their belief that Harry was possessed, even in the face of the hospital's evidence of his illness. The third and final world-view is symbolic and metaphorical. An individual operating with this world-view 'retains the language of myth, the anthropomorphic image, the historical setting, because without them he or she has no language at all with which to speak about ultimate concern'. The chaplain in the 'Faith and Doubt' group takes the story of Nicodemus with Jesus. Jesus, according to St John, uses the image of rebirth symbolically, and Nicodemus thinks he is speaking literally. The authors further suggest that the kind of pastoral care appropriate to each of these world-views is different. Pastoral care for the people holding the first is best expressed by passively being with them, the second by a more active approach of doing things with them, and the third by a more mutual sharing and exploring together. For a fuller picture of the stages of faith, see J. W. Fowler, *Stages of Faith* (Harper Row, New York, 1981).
7. See Chapter 7, pp. 139–40: Senile dementia.

Further reading

Goffman, E., *Asylums.* Penguin 1961.
Menzies, I., *Social Systems as a Defence Against Anxiety.* Tavistock Institute 1970.
Reed, B., *The Dynamics of Religion.* Darton Longman and Todd 1978.

FOUR

Revealing the Meaning in 'Madness'

> It is a remarkable fact that when, in modern novels, for instance, the misery of people with weak personalities is described, it is always the key words of mysticism that are used. But what are virtues for the mystic are torment and sickness for the modern man or woman; estrangement, loneliness, silence, solitude, inner emptiness, deprivation, poverty, not-knowing and so forth. . . What the monks sought for in order to find God, modern men and women fly from as if it were the devil. Earlier mystics withdrew into the loneliness of the desert in order to fight with demons and to experience Christ's victory over them. It seems to me today that we need people who are prepared to enter in the inner wilderness of the soul and wander through the abysses of the self in order to fight with demons and to experience Christ's victory there . . .[1]

The search for meaning in madness requires extraordinary commitment, and a personal need which can be neither denied nor avoided. It has about it all the characteristics of a 'vocation', a calling which demands a following. Many of us take up the call, at least for a brief exploration here or there, but the horrors and demands of the journey force us to beat a hasty retreat. People learn to make what they can of their ways of coping, sensing that, although the mystery of suffering could reveal more, the cost is too much and the need not quite enough to spur them on.

Perhaps one of life's crises catches us off our guard, and we are precipitated headlong into the jungle or desert. There we are left to find our way out, or to settle for a life of relative misery, eased somewhat by the physician's potions and the carer's sympathy. Yet there are explorers, the committed who take up their crosses and find unknown resources within themselves, and within those, their counsellors, whom they choose to accompany them.

Pastoral counselling, as well as being a technique and perspective which enables pastor and pastored to overcome or cope with the ordinary ups and downs of life, is also a way of discovering meaning in life itself. The odds and ends of meaning revealed in the short and often chance conversations of Chapter 2 can, if they are attended to, lead like a trail to more and more meanings. In this chapter it is the trail of 'madness' itself which we will follow. Three people share their experience of 'madness' in some detail and depth. First is the record of a pastoral counsellor's work with David, followed by accounts from Leslie and Mary of what they learnt from their illnesses. Both are transcriptions of interviews with them, which were recorded and edited. For all three it was their need and their commitment which took them deep into their 'madness'. Their suffering would not leave them alone, but drove them to search for meaning, and to accept their experience as an essential part of their vocation.

David

I first met David because of my involvement with another patient's death and funeral. He asked if he might talk to me, because he felt that I could help him. In the course of conversations he told me about his life and particularly the recent experiences which had brought him into hospital. For as long as he could remember he had felt the need and the ability to love others. He said, rather shyly, 'In the way Christ meant we should love others'. Some ten years previously he had had the opportunity to do this in a very practical way. He found himself at the centre of a local community association which fought and won a series of battles against the giants of society. Much was achieved for and by ordinary people. He became more and more committed, and more and more important to this community and its ideals. He can sense now how close he was to a kind of fanaticism, and yet at the time it was a liberating and fulfilling occupation. He knew that it was right and that he was right to be doing it. Gradually he became aware that he and the community were being exploited by some members of the association. Suddenly everything began to crumble. Trust was destroyed and he felt betrayed. Love and morality, as he understood it, were turned on their head. His own love swung dramatically to hate. Where he had built he now wanted to pull down and, because of his destructiveness, he came first into the courts and then into hospital. The challenge he threw at me was, 'What about your Christianity? I actually lived it and look what has happened.' He did not want to hear about turning the other cheek. He wanted most of all to be believed, and for me to show him where he had deceived himself, and so engineered this catastrophe. Had he got Christianity wrong or was it fundamentally wrong in any case? Or had this been due to an illness, a 'madness' which governed his life and from which he could not escape?

It was to these questions and others like them that we addressed our search. At first he thought that I must have the answers, and was frustrated when I did not give them. Gradually we each came to recognize that the answers, if there were any, lay ahead of us, and that together we could go and look for them; or as he once said at the end of an interview, 'I don't have to go on with this, do I?' 'No,' I replied, 'the choice is always yours.'

This first conversation comes from early in our meetings when David talked of the prison, in which he was both being kept and keeping himself. Was it some kind of punishment for what had happened, or was it the only safe place in which to be?

DAVID: Oh yes, people say, do-gooders say, stick in the middle, but I can't, I just can't. I've built a wall round me ten feet thick, and I won't come out.

COUNSELLOR: What's it like in there?

DAVID: Terrible. I'm holding on to the bars screaming, but I don't want to come out. Outside could be even worse. Once bitten you know . . . then all dogs, all people are my enemies.

COUNSELLOR: You are too hurt . . . too vulnerable.

DAVID: Vulnerable, that's a good word. And I hate me and all those people. The ones I worked for. I want them to suffer and to take away all that I got for them. To put them back where they were before.

He went on to describe his work with the association, and how it had started and what had been achieved. I asked him what he felt had motivated him to give so much. He thought for a while and then told me about his experience of the school he went to when he was eight. He recalled being a very miserable, wet and snivelling child, overwhelmed by a mother who was fixated with him, and distant from an undemonstrative and withdrawn father. He was sent to boarding-school, which, to his utter amazement, accepted him, weak and ineffective as he was. For the first time in his life he felt valued rather than possessed or ignored. He learnt what it was to be loved and to love, not in sentimental and weak ways, but strongly and realistically. As he talked he began to cry, and he wanted me to know that his tears were a mixture of sadness and joy, gratitude and anger.

DAVID: They made me, of all the places I have been to, that place made me what I am.

COUNSELLOR: So that explains something. The two you's, one the snivelling infant, and the other the child who responded to that school and was loved by it. Was that split very difficult for you? School so good and home so bad; I wonder if you felt disloyal?

DAVID: Oh yes, very disloyal and guilty. My mother and father were so different, they fought a great deal. She always noisily and hysterically, and he withdrawn and sulking. They stayed together for me. How dreadful, when I wanted nothing more than that they should be apart!

COUNSELLOR: That was very hard for you, and what a contrast to your school.

DAVID (*crying*): Yes and it wasn't weak. It was tough and real, it gave us rules and guidance.

COUNSELLOR: Something you could be sure of, and know where you were with it.

(*David nods and cries again.*)

COUNSELLOR: David, do you remember when first you were aware of that conflict between your parents, or between your experience of home and school?

DAVID (*stirring himself*): Yes, very clearly. I can't think how old I was, but quite little, perhaps two. My father took me out in his car. He must have sat me on the front seat, and it was dark or nearly dark. I remember all the lights as we sped past them. I was excited, not frightened, but really exhilarated. There was no experience like it. When we got home my mother was furious. She blamed my father, I suppose because she thought it was dangerous. I couldn't understand why she was like that, and I expected my father to explain how wonderful and good it had been. But he didn't say anything.

Often we have returned to that car journey, to a child whose most wonderful experience was so fundamentally challenged by his parents' reaction to it, and whose sense of moral outrage and conflict was so early invoked. His whole being could not allow what had been so good to be judged and accepted as so bad, his disappointment with his father competing with his horror at his mother. Who was right and who was wrong?[2] The battle of good and evil has raged on in and around David ever since, as though reconciliation is not possible, only the defeat of one and the ultimate victory of the other. It was some time before an event in David's life produced a different perspective to that of ultimate conflict. He came to one of our meetings looking very different and began:

DAVID: I want to tell you about something very wonderful, it's incredible . . .

COUNSELLOR: Mm.

DAVID: You remember I told you about Mike (*his lover of some years earlier*), who I lived with . . . and who I threw out. God, I was a bastard. I turned on him and of course he went. He couldn't understand what was happening, poor kid. I remember his face, his pleading, but he went. Then I tried to reach him, to put it right, and I couldn't find him. He disappeared over two years ago. Well, he wrote to me, a letter came last week. I couldn't believe it, the poor little bugger. He actually apologized for bothering me again. He apologized to me. Then he phoned, he's so impetuous, the opposite of me. He said that he'd come right away on a plane. He'd no money, anyway the details don't matter. He just came.

COUNSELLOR: Mm.

DAVID: He came from the airport by taxi and he rushed over to greet me and embraced me there . . . He didn't worry about the people or the taxi-driver. He was shaking and so scared, the poor little devil. Oh God, what I did to him, how could I? Anyway we came inside the house. He had changed, he wasn't as young, but then so had I. I made us sit down and look at one another face to face. To see what we were like. He was so frightened. I suppose he thought that I wouldn't like him anymore. He's not so attractive, that's true, but then neither am I. But I do love him . . . Look, oh God, look at what he's done, what he's gone through. The bloody courage of it . . . I don't know what is happening to me . . .

COUNSELLOR: You're really frightened too?

DAVID: Yes, that's it. I'm scared stiff, and so excited. I'm thinking about going back to him now . . . (*Pause.*) I thought a lot about you this week. As though I can believe in God again. God, who I rejected, who I gave up on. If God is love and love is God. You see I do love him. I never knew before, but I do now; God I'm scared.

COUNSELLOR: Scared of what you've found and what it means?

DAVID: Yes, frightened stiff. I never told him I loved him; he always did, but I couldn't. Now I can.

COUNSELLOR: So he's taught you something?

DAVID: What?

COUNSELLOR: He's taught you about losing. That, paradoxically, impossibly, losing something or someone is how we find something. Losing him uncovered your love for him.

DAVID: My God, that's right . . . He has taught me a lot. I've got all this head stuff, but he teaches me about my heart and my guts and yes, my genitals.

COUNSELLOR: It sounds as though there is a crack in your wall.

DAVID: I thought about that too. This is being, I'm real for once. God, it scares me.

I remember shaking myself as I withdrew from this meeting. The echoes of prodigal sons, of losing in order to find, and dying in order to live, were so clear and so close, the 'holiness' of the experience was awe-inspiring. It is difficult to convey in words what appeared to be happening. The battling parts of David had found some harmony for once, mind and body were not trying to beat each other, and as a consequence he felt real. Also he knew inside himself something which I had tried and failed to convey, either by what I did or said. For him, good and evil were inextricably locked in mortal conflict, there was no way that he could see how badness could be accepted, let alone loved. That, for him, was typical of mealy-mouthed Christians. Mike's return, and all that happened as a result of it, called in question the conflict of good and evil and introduced, as nothing else could, the experience of forgiveness and of grace. David got what he did not deserve and for once he could dare to let himself have it.

Some weeks later the relationship between David and Mike came to another destructive and abrupt end. David was distraught beyond words at what he had done, but with a difference. It was what *he* had done; he felt again in possession, if not totally in command, of himself. He had touched upon his capacity to love and to be loved for love's sake, and not because of some debt that he owed the school which had loved him and which he needed to repay. As he said, 'It's simply a matter of God being love and love being God.'

David is not sure when the change came about, but he did begin to take up again his personal responsibilities, first for his home, and then for leaving hospital and thinking about work, and perhaps, most symbolically, by getting his body back into shape. He returned to his gymnasium for weight-lifting. In the last two months he has talked very differently about himself – of someone who is alive again, who is frightened of what he has been through and fears falling back into, and yet whose strength and confidence grows with each day of being better. The last conversation recorded here captures again his struggle with the mystery of what we can do for ourselves and what we have to await happening within us. Our health is a mixture of the active and the passive.

DAVID: I remember my teacher at drama school saying that you could prepare yourself so far and do so much, but then you had to launch out, push the boat out – let yourself go. That's what I can't do, and it makes me so fucking annoyed. I go round and round, thinking about it, and then I tell myself to stop thinking any more. But it's my bloody mind who's telling me. Do you see I can't get away from it.

COUNSELLOR: What prevents you launching out?

DAVID: What prevents me? . . . I don't know . . . I suppose I'm frightened.

COUNSELLOR: Frightened of what?

DAVID: Yes, what am I frightened of? . . . That really is strange. I've not thought of that before. I'm frightened of showing myself. Yes, of being exposed. It reminds me of being at school, little and spotty and bullied, as though that's how I would be seen. That's odd, because I don't mind being seen now, you know, as I am now.

COUNSELLOR: Yet when you 'launched out' by going back to the gym, you did have that fear. What they might think about you and how you looked. You felt you had to creep in.

DAVID: Oh yes. I hadn't connected that.

COUNSELLOR: So it's when you anticipate, or come near to launching out, that your fear of being that spotty child is activated and your mind protects you from that feeling. But once you let yourself go, it's all right.

DAVID: Mm. (*He thinks for a while.*) I go four times a week now, and it's good. I'm so much fitter, but also it stops my brain. I can really concentrate on the effort of it, like having a donkey brain.

COUNSELLOR: A donkey brain. What do you mean?

DAVID: Well, like a donkey pulling a load, not distracted by anything else. I stop thinking about being and just am. That's it. I want to be, and I need my guts just to be. That has always been my trouble, that my brain is so good and bright. I don't want to reject it, but my guts are good too. I need them to have a chance for a change. It's as if they have come out, and they are saying, 'Look at me, I'm bloody good too, and I'm creative and alive'. And I look at them and say, 'That's right, you are bloody good too.'

COUNSELLOR (*smiling*): Mm.

DAVID (*smiling and waving his hands and legs*): Yes, you see, here they are now, alive and active, that's what I want.

It is nearly a year since the last of those conversations. David, by his standards, is unbelievably better. He has come out of his prison. Now the conflicts, the different parts and people, the snivelling and strong child, his mind and body, live in greater harmony with one another. There are still setbacks, a rejection here, a failure to live up to his own expectations of himself there. These things take their toll, but he has found that he can ride out the storms. In his words, he is no longer the two-year-old sitting beside his father in the passenger seat. He is the driver now, who occasionally drops in to invite me out for a ride.

Leslie

Leslie is a middle-aged man who has a long history of depression, including a number of admissions to a psychiatric hospital and regular out-patient treatment over a number of years. He records here what that illness was like for him, how his developing faith as a Christian altered that and, by implication, how those who gave him pastoral counselling contributed to that change.

When you are depressed, or when I am depressed, I am paralyzed and cannot think constructively or creatively. I have no confidence in myself and so I withdraw more and more from people. I feel worthless and useless, and I am convinced that this is going to be permanent. Even the smallest things and decisions make me very anxious and unsure. In particular I don't know what I am going to say to people who approach me. I remember this all beginning, when suddenly that feeling left me.

One day I was coming home on the bus and travelling with a neighbour whom I knew well, and he was easy to be with. But there was a stranger there as well and he introduced me to him, and that began to make me very anxious. We got off the bus and it was a long walk to our homes, and I just didn't know how I was going to take part in the conversation. Then, all of a sudden, I had a feeling of well-being, which I had never experienced before. It is very difficult to describe, but a pleasant feeling, as though someone was around me, and a strong sense of goodwill. My anxiety left me and I felt secure. The conversation between the two carried on, and I was no longer anxious even though I wasn't taking part. I didn't think any more about it until a couple of hours later when all sorts of religious phrases began coming into my mind, some were vaguely familiar and others completely new. One thought I had was that all the good things come from God and all the bad from the devil, and I knew that now I could believe. I think what had always prevented me from believing was that there was so much evil in the world, I couldn't believe there could be a God who cares for us.

This same feeling came again. And one thing about it was the sense of being controlled. I wasn't controlling things any more, but everything was being controlled in some way that made me feel safe. And looking back I see from my diary that I wrote at that time, 'Have I had a religious experience?' I remember I began to pray and to read the Bible, but I wasn't going to church. So I began by telling my family about it. My son was a Christian and I went to my first service on Good Friday and then again on the Sunday. Two months later I decided I should go and talk to somebody about it, and I went to see the hospital chaplain. I told him the story and said that I had come to him for further guidance. I was surprised by his reaction. He didn't try to influence me, I suppose I expected him to preach or something, but what he said was: 'So far this experience has brought you here, let's see where it takes you.' That released a lot of questions in me, and we talked on a number of occasions. I knew I wanted to be a member of the Church of England. I am not sure why, and he told me about the other denominations, but I knew it was the Church of England I wanted to join. I think it attracted me because it was more tolerant and free, and I have always been a very independent thinker. The chaplain suggested that I go to visit a local church, which he knew of; he contacted the vicar. I can clearly remember the first Sunday I went to that church. The vicar came towards me outside the church with his hand stretched out to greet me. They made me feel very at home, like joining a family who cared about me.

Later, when I was ill again, a number of people from this congregation, some of whom I didn't know very well, came to see me in hospital, and when I returned to the church I was welcomed back. I remember feeling how wonderful that was, a real sense of belonging to a family. I felt accepted for myself as I was; when you get these depressions you feel you are not worth accepting. If a person comes up to you and says something complimentary you tend to feel he is only just doing that to cheer you up, he doesn't mean it. When you are feeling worthless, that is how you take it. When something comes from outside like an unseen hand, you can't say that about it.

At the beginning I was praying a great deal because I was anxious about so many things. I felt my prayers were not being answered, because I had failed to deal with a specific problem. I think that if I had more faith in God to work things out, I wouldn't have got so ill again. I read somewhere in one of the prophets: 'Be still and know that I am God.' Sometimes if you feel you can't control events, if you can be still, then God will. As it happened, the problem I was worried about got better by itself, while I was in hospital unable to do anything about it. Since then I have had things which have brought me very low, but I have found, by being prepared to wait for God, I've been able to keep going. It is easier now to understand the purpose of suffering because it has been answered by my own personal suffering. I spoke to a patient who was a Baptist, and whose answers to my questions were so helpful. He said that we were often not aware of the reasons for our suffering. You can be suffering to help others, as Jesus did, or it can be used to correct or show where you are at fault; without the suffering you wouldn't be able to tell. I mean, only the other day somebody asked about the tragedy in Italy and why God allows such cruel things. I didn't know the answer to that one. Suffering comes for a reason and won't last for ever, that's what I feel now. It is like being born again, because when you get into a depression it's like death, you are not active any more. When you come out of it you start afresh, and if you've learnt something during the course of the depression you have something with which to start anew.

It isn't easy to practise Christianity in hospital among very disturbed and sometimes violent people. In a Christian community it's different, with people who are friendly and gentle. When you are up against violence and anger and hate, and you get angry, you feel a failure. One just has to keep trying. Some of the staff are very helpful, but not all are. Those who help are those who give the impression of caring about you as an individual. You are not just another patient, you are a person to them.

Leslie's journey has moved on considerably from the point at which he shared these thoughts. He has managed good and bad times, recognizing that in the bad ones there is a kind of dying in order to be born again. And that depression as well as being an illness is also the internal working out of something vital to the spirit. His gifts as a writer and a speaker led him into the local amateur dramatic company, where, no longer tongue-tied, he acts before large audiences. Spurred on by his success he began to train as a lay-reader and has now received his licence. He preaches regularly in his local church, and recently at the harvest festival service in the hospital, where he was once a patient, he had this to say: 'When I was a patient here, little did I imagine that six years later I would be preaching in this hospital chapel, which just goes to show that in God's hands you never know what the future has in store for you! As I stand here this evening, as a licenced reader, I am reaping the harvest of the seed that was sown at that time.'

Mary

Mary is a nun who spent two years in a psychiatric hospital suffering from depression. She received a whole range of treatments including electro-convulsive therapy (ECT), behaviour therapy and psychotherapy.[3] She was also visited by three chaplains, two of her own denomination and one of another. She kept a diary while she was in hospital, and then recorded her reactions to the whole experience some two years later. She included her feelings about her family, her order and her religion. The following is an edited selection from that diary and that recording under various headings.

The illness

— is like hell

I wish with every nerve of my body and every fibre of my being that I did not exist, if only I could shut my eyes and just fade out of existence. Nobody knows that every second round of the clock is hell shouting in my head. I'm sure that no one, but no one, can come on into the inside to understand what it feels like. Neither can they get a grip of it and pull me out. It's mine, all mine, and I feel the only answer I have is to hide away with it; but if I went into outer space, it could not be far enough away from people. In all this ugly mess there is very little I can identify or recognize. It is just a heap of muck. I wish the doctor was invincible enough to disperse it, but it would be like trying to empty an ocean of sludge with a teaspoon.

— isolates

I really was afraid to let anyone know what was happening. I didn't understand it, and no one else seemed to understand it. And I was afraid that if I tried to tell anyone, that I'd be really very disappointed and that it would confirm the isolation that I felt.

— panic

I went through panic sessions, everybody seemed to me to be my enemy. I don't know what I thought they were going to do to me. But I was afraid to go over to them, and I was feeling very bad.

— is it real?
I never could judge how ill I had to be in order to say I was ill. I'd sit for hours thinking: 'Perhaps I should tell them, perhaps I shouldn't.' I sensed they were angry with me and that made it worse.

— no control
I had no control over anything. I think that was the most frightening thing of all. I couldn't control myself from running off, I couldn't control the bad feelings. I think that was really frightening, to be totally without any control over any of the events inside or outside me.

— little things
I realize that when one small thing in my environment makes me feel bad, I generalize it and feel totally criticized. That makes me want to disappear. I lump everything together as though there is nothing around affirming me.

— ending it all
I was probably closest to suicide when I nearly walked in front of a car. I was shopping and suddenly it seemed to me it would be all peaceful and quiet. It was just a thought, there was no conflict: 'I could step in front of that car and it would all be over.' It wasn't until an hour later that I realized how close I had been. Perhaps that is the nearest to what suicide is like, I don't know. It would have been a quite happy moment really.

— never the same again
I feel I'm probably through the black tunnel. I pray it will never return. I can't be absolutely sure, but at least I feel fairly hopeful. I'm not the only one who has had a rotten time of it. I'm sure I gave everyone round me a rotten time. Maybe there is a future for me with others now, I hope I use it well. I can never take anything for granted again. I've been so close to hell.

Treatment

— is it really necessary?
The first doctor I saw said to me: 'You're going to have to come into hospital. You're really quite badly ill.' My superior said: 'You know there is nothing wrong with you. If you weren't so self-absorbed, and so selfish, you'd snap out of this.' And I sat there in absolute disbelief.

The doctor threatened to slap a section on me. I think that was how she managed to get through to us, that she considered me to be very ill indeed.

— being in hospital
I look back over my stay in hospital and I can still say, even now: 'I hated that place.' I saw the hospital as a very pagan place, because it gave me no Christianity, nothing in a Christian way.

— asking for help
If I didn't go and ask for help, there was the chance that some help was there. If I went and asked for it and I only got all this waffle [psychotherapy], then there was no help and I might as well be dead.

— psychotherapy[3]
I don't think any therapy justifies leaving people feeling as ill as I felt over as long a period, in the hope that in three or four years time I would understand it all. It doesn't seem justifiable, perhaps the selection of me for that kind of treatment was wrong.

— behaviour therapy[3]
I think when I first came in the doctor took control, because I was on a behavioural programme. He was a brute about it, but I had to do it and so was very controlled. I think I felt more secure than later when I was in the psychotherapy unit. There wasn't that kind of control, it seemed to me as though they did not know what they were doing.

— ECT[3]
It was virtually useless as far as I was concerned. I'd never be

afraid of it really. I used to look forward to it in a sense, because at least I knew I would sleep for an hour afterwards. When it was first suggested I felt so rotten that I really didn't care what I signed.

– drugs
They would say to me: 'Now we are going to try you on something new, as you haven't responded to the others. We really feel that perhaps this will do it.' I hoped they were right, but then I was let down when it didn't work. I think I became fairly cynical about their drugs. But then I got resentful when they took them away and wouldn't let me have anything to help when I felt so bad.

What made the difference
I couldn't change anything, and I found that quite frightening because I couldn't see how I could get better unless I had some control in the affairs. I think it was probably wrong. One of the psychotherapists said to me: 'It's only by completely giving up control that you are going to get better.' I think he was right, because that is what actually happened. I did not choose to give up, but I got too ill to attempt any control; and I think it was when I gave up all attempts that I began to get better.

I remember the therapist telling me: 'You've got to let yourself get as bad as you possibly can, and stop fighting it.' I said: 'If I do that I'm going to go completely mad. I could become so ill that I would never get better. What guarantee can you give me that that won't happen?' 'None,' he said, 'that's the risk you take.' I said, 'You must be joking, that's too great a risk for anyone to take. I'm going to get myself better.' But I reckon he was right. It was as though I had battled for seven or eight years to stop the illness conquering me, and I'd given up the battle only to find that the illness could not defeat me, that I could in fact beat the illness, but by peaceful means. Perhaps the fight was important too. Certainly I don't think I would have learnt so much if I hadn't gone right through the whole experience.

I discovered I could be very ill indeed and still be rational. There's that small part of yourself that is rational, that knows why you are behaving so strangely. You can understand, even if others can't. I feel that in hospital they should talk to that part of the person that is still functioning. I think they tend to talk just to the ill part. They could have helped the part of me that was well to help the part that was ill.

The family

I wouldn't go near the doctor because I felt that once I went, I might have to tell my family, 'I'm ill'. I don't know what it was but I could not tell them, and it was worse because it was a mental illness.

My sister's response was: 'We've known for a long time that something must be wrong, so for God's sake go to a doctor.' When my mother rang up, I fainted on the phone, and the strange thing is that we have never talked about it (my illness). They asked me how I was and I would say, 'Fine', having had an absolutely filthy and awful week. To this day we have never discussed it. I think I tried to keep them out of it, because I thought they wouldn't understand at an emotional level. We just were never ill in our family.

When I ran away from hospital my sister said: 'Well, come and sleep the night and think about it in the morning.' I was glad when she took over like that, that was the role I wanted her to play.

The order and the church

I've had people in the order say to me: 'I couldn't face the fact that you were ill.' They just wouldn't accept it, and I felt that very keenly.

I suppose they thought that if it had happened to me, then none of them were safe. For some it was frightening for themselves. Others were too angry to come and see me, some of them have expressed that. Others were guilty that they had failed to pick up the signs, and it was their fault. One of the hardest things was that they didn't visit me.

The local church was an escape from the hospital, my little bit of Christianity. I remember once, some nuns were there. I went to kneel beside them for communion. I wasn't in my habit, and I thought, 'You don't know that I am a nun, but it's important for me that I'm with you because that's what I am. It is right for me to be with a group of nuns.' When they left I remember thinking, 'I'm here on my own, I'm not with my community, but this is universal, this is sharing anyway.'

As far as the hospital was concerned the church was really a dead loss. I remember thinking that I should write to the bishop and say, 'The people in this hospital must be so important to Christ, and you're not reaching them. Not because of bad will or anything like that, but because the whole system is so cock-eyed.'

On one or two occasions that I did get over to the Bible study, it was a relief. Just to be in a different group, a relief to be in a Christian group.

Prayer and worship

I went to the psalms that seemed to speak loudest about how I was feeling, because they had expressed a lot of it. And I found it very hard, because they reflected so accurately what I was feeling. During the Good Friday office I was just sitting there crying right the way through, thinking, 'Well, everyone is tripping these things off their tongues, but what do you do when it's you?'

I used to think, 'I'm a totally bad Christian.'

I sat in the Mass very often and just hung it out. I'd say, 'I'm here, I've got nothing to give. Empty hands is all you've got, and can I have something back in return? Make it good if you can.'

Sermons made me angry, and a religious tape that spoke about the joy of suffering. I switched it off. What in God's name did they think they were talking about? If there was any joy, there wouldn't be any suffering.

I felt people thinking, 'If only you prayed, and if only you trusted, and if only you believed in the mercy of God, then you would be fine.' I'm sure that was wrong, but that's what I picked up.

The pastors

The priests were totally confused, but I don't think that was their fault. They didn't know what to do with our problems.

One saw me as someone who was well and didn't see the illness at all. Perhaps I didn't show it to him, because he would talk to me as though I was at work. I didn't get anything from him apart from going to confession, when he was really very kind. It was important that the priest, who heard my confession, was able to recognize my inability to separate what was illness and what was badness. He was able to do that by giving me absolution and saying, 'I absolve you, and don't be pulling yourself apart.' The other priest was even better, he was able to recognize my feelings and talk about them more, and give me a general absolution.

My sacramental life was really important to me, and that the Anglican chaplain couldn't give me, although he was important as the one bit of Christianity that was a part of the hospital. He was the one Christian person in this unchristian place. I think that helped me come in touch with my own Christian self. I felt such a bad Christian, but his coming meant that I wasn't such a total write-off, and that a lot of my experiences were common to Christians. He actually quietened my soul down.

He was able to help me sort out what was going on, so that I didn't despair of my interactions with the staff and other patients. He helped me stand back from it, and look at it from another point of view. That was more the counselling role.

The pastoring that would have helped

I think I would have welcomed the chaplain talking about prayer, but in another sense I probably wasn't ready. I felt so badly about my prayer, that to have talked about it would have high-lighted what I couldn't do. I think it would have helped if he had taken the initiative, and helped me use my uselessness. I found it very confusing, I think I was aware for the first time how conservative a Catholic I am. To me it's very strange to discuss prayer and religion with someone who isn't a Catholic.

I think what would have helped would have been to link my feelings to some spiritual part of me and say, 'Well, that's where you are at the moment, I don't understand it but I offer it.' Something quite simple like that would have helped a lot. A kind of, 'Yes, it's all right to do it that way.'

I wanted to know it was all right to shut my ears to the readings when they were too painful, and what to do when I felt so angry with people that I couldn't be a Christian. If I could have had that help without it being preaching on suffering, that would have meant a lot.

When I couldn't do anything, I wanted them [the priests] to say, 'What's so bad about sitting in church feeling awful?' I don't think I had anyone who could sit with me where I was spiritually.

Vocation

I never knew how much God would have wanted me to suffer, and I used to wonder if perhaps, my tolerance was very low. Would God say: 'You didn't last very long. You had a fairly good life really, and I gave you this thing, and you chucked it in.' I felt I didn't have the right to intervene and take my life. I had this strong conviction that that was not a choice open to me. I think that was my own personal faith. I just remember sitting there and I started to cry, and I couldn't stop. I thought, 'Really I'm the only person in this room [psychotherapy group] who has vowed total commitment and I'm unable to be totally committed to anything. I'm the person who is committed and I'm not fulfilling my commitment.'

The chaplain said he wondered if my illness was a kind of vocation. I think it was a pity that I didn't capitalize on that, for my own spiritual advancement. It was a pity too, that he didn't go further with it; but I don't think that would have been possible either, because the whole experience was one of non-achievement. For anyone to have said they thought I was achieving something would have meant that they did not understand what I was feeling.

Mary's description of her 'illness', treatment and care affords us a vivid picture of the cost of suffering, and of pastor and pastored watching and waiting for healing and salvation. Mary can now appreciate the paradox in which she and her family, her order and her helpers found themselves. She and they were wanting, more than anything else, to be close enough to one another to be some help and consolation, and yet they were being driven apart by the horror and intensity of what was happening. 'I'm sure that no one, but no one, can come on into the inside to understand what this feels like. Neither can they get a grip of it and pull me out . . .' There was no short cut, no miracle to ease the passage or shorten the journey. On the one hand, Mary wanted her pastors to be with her spiritually, on the other she could not let them near her. She remembers one hour of psychotherapy, when she was at her worst, and completely unable to speak. The therapist said to her, that he sensed her condition and that all he could offer was to sit with her in silence for that hour. Later she said it reminded her of Christ in the garden of Gethsemane, wanting his friends just to watch with him. 'That was what I needed, but I didn't know at the time, and so I couldn't ask for it.'

Mary is now back with her community and working as an educational psychologist. Recently, speaking at a meeting about the 'Church' within the psychiatric hospital, she talked of her frantic search for it, the more so as she failed to find it. 'The hospital gave me no Christianity.' Ironically she eventually discovered it where she least expected to, within herself. As she grew better, she was approached by other patients, 'They gave me my ministry back, they helped me find something inside me which I thought had died.' So too, she can now see more clearly the relationship between her treatment, which she hated so much, and her own spiritual journey. We have grown so used to equating our religion with good and positive feelings, that we can see no place in it for the bad and negative. Such things must be overcome or exorcised and, if that fails, then it is we who are beyond the pale. And yet the biblical witness, in the Psalms, Jeremiah and Job, the passion narratives and the epistles, is inclusive of the very worst in human experience. That too can be offered to God, and God found within it.

To continue the quotation with which this chapter started:

> It seems to me that today we need people to enter into the inner wilderness of the soul . . . in order to fight with demons, and to experience Christ's victory there, or simply in order to make an inner space for living possible, and to open up a way of escape for other people through spiritual experience. And in our context that means wresting a

positive meaning out of the loneliness, the silence, the inner emptiness, the suffering, the poverty, the spiritual dryness and 'the knowledge that knows nothing'. The mystics experience this meaning in the form of a paradox. For them, it meant learning to live in the absence of God who is present, or in the presence of God who is absent, and enduring what St John of the Cross called the 'dark night of the soul'. Can it still mean that today?[4]

Notes

1. Moltmann, *Experiences of God,* SCM Press, 1980; see p. 61.
2. Isaiah 5.20.
3. See Chapter 7: p. 129, Electro-convulsive therapy; p. 132, Psychotherapy; and pp. 132–3, Behaviour therapy.
4. Moltmann, op. cit.

Further reading

Axline, V. M., *Dibs: in Search of Self.* Penguin 1966.
Barnes, M. and Berke, J., *Mary Barnes: Two Accounts of a Journey through Madness.* Penguin 1973.
Green, H., *I Never Promised You a Rose Garden.* Pan 1967.
Rowe, D., *Depression: the Way Out of Your Prison.* Routledge and Kegan Paul 1983 (MIND Book of the Year).
Storr, A., *The Integrity of the Personality.* Penguin 1963.

Part Two

FIVE

Knowing Oneself

For now we see in a mirror dimly, but then face to face. Now I know in part; then I shall understand fully, even as I have been fully understood.[1]

He never would have become the productive chaplain if he had not been familiar with the world of his patient through his own experience. Even after his breakdown he remained a patient and suffered from the basic conflicts involved all through his life. But his own sufferings offered him the core insights of the clinical training movement, and became the source of inspiration for new views in the psychology of religion.[2]

This is how Henri Nouwen has described Anton Boisen, who was a psychiatric patient and then a chaplain in the same hospital. In his book *The Wounded Healer*, Nouwen expresses a conviction similar to the one he recognized in Anton Boisen. We can only understand others in so far as we can understand ourselves. In some mysterious way it is our wounds which provide the richest resource for our work as helpers and healers. Boisen went further in claiming that we are 'living human documents' of the Gospel, comparable in our significance to the biblical documents, which were being so vigorously examined at the same time as he began his study of himself and others. Just as the passion narratives were central to much biblical criticism so the human passion was the focus of his study.

Important as self-knowledge is, it is neither easily won or readily used. As described in Chapter 4, David, Leslie and Mary reveal the enormous hazards and obstacles which they encountered on their journey inwards. There are additional and complex problems for those who are drawn to helping others, and whose own journey can so easily become confused with the journeys of those they try to help.

First the personal needs and wounds of the helper may not be so immediate and so intense as those who seek their help. Such counsellors will have difficulty grasping the degree of distress in others, whose life experience has been so much worse than theirs. They will need help to find in their own suffering at least a pale reflection of other people's pain, and the courage to meet and not be overwhelmed by the envy they evoke. They will often be unrealistically optimistic and hopeful in the face of despair and pessimism or, like the chaplain who visited Edward,[3] they will do their best to explain what is wrong from their own point of view, unaware of how different that perspective may be.

Other helpers will be inclined to repress or hide from their needs and wounds. Indeed their involvement in pastoral counselling may arise in part from their inability to face in themselves what they meet in others. All will be well until the level of distress they encounter stirs up feelings in themselves which they can no longer control and, like an exploding volcano, their repression bursts and their cover is blown. The high incidence of sudden breakdown or break out among helpers suggests that is what sometimes happens.[4] Alternatively, counsellors may project their needs onto or into those who come to them for help and, by caring for others, vicariously care for themselves. Once the respective needs of helper and helped diverge, as they usually do, then both are left with a sense of betrayal and confusion. Harry's illness[5] exposed the fear of 'madness' in his family and church, and the fear of religion in the hospital staff. Little could be done for Harry until each had taken some care of their own fears.

The selection and training of people for many of the helping professions often includes attention to the development of self-understanding, in order to minimize the detrimental effects we can have upon others and to maximize the positive contribution we want to make. Counsellors, for instance, are usually expected to have been counselled themselves before they begin counselling others. Not that they should be healed of all their infirmities, but in order that they recognize and appreciate how their infirmities will influence their work for good and ill.

Experience suggests that pastoral counsellors are vulnerable in particular areas. Hugh Eadie's study of Scottish clergy revealed that pastors find their sexual and aggressive feelings the most difficult to manage.

> Therefore, [he concludes] any wishes, feelings or needs associated with these life forces are particularly conducive of anxiety and guilt in the clergyman. One of the principal costs of the clergyman's compulsive attempts to be lovable is that he should appear to be asexual and non-aggressive . . . The basic point is that the clergyman has a compulsive need to reject erotic and aggressive anger in himself and others . . . Only the most perceptive observer or his closest intimates may be aware of the internal conflicts and anxiety to which the clergyman is prone.[6]

Counselling itself may be an attempt to overcome that conflict, to understand and accept in others what the counsellor can not accept in himself. Although some things may be gained from such vicarious attempts at self-healing, more often neither counsellor nor counselled are helped. As well as sexual and aggressive feelings, doubt and despair, and lack of faith and commitment[7] can be equally difficult, as can the kind of temptations recorded in the story of Jesus in the wilderness. The need to be omnipotent and omniscient can create enormous burdens for pastors and for those upon whom they inevitably lean.

There is a great deal in the pastoral counsellor's own personality, and in the expectations which come from religious and secular traditions, to prevent proper and adequate self-scrutiny. For instance, such loving of oneself is, according to much of the church's teaching, indulgent and profitless, if not downright sinful. It takes a great deal to overcome such barriers to a thorough-going and constructive self-understanding. We need much patience with ourselves and our colleagues to help us understand such a venture, and then to continue with it as we begin to face the worst about ourselves. Indeed, it will not be unlike the experiences of the wilderness and the dark night of the soul. Journeys inwards of this kind and importance cry out for good preparation, and the right companionship of spiritual director, therapist or counsellor.

There is something to be gained from all the traditions of self-examination, and more from a recognition of their shared features than from their differing ideologies. Spiritual direction, counselling and therapy all give particular importance to certain things. They stress the value of regular time, space and opportunity within a secure relationship, as the prerequisite of any serious self-exploration. We need someone or some group of people, to whom we can turn, not only in crisis (crises are often a distraction), but regularly to share our journey inwards. The more regular the time, space and opportunity, the more consistent the relationship, the more honest and far-reaching the exploration will be. Different traditions, be they spiritual or psychological, assume the regular setting aside of time for self-examination. The medium used may be our dreams, bodily and physical reactions, significant relationships or our prayers. Any of these can help to unearth what lies hidden, unexpressed and unaccepted. The qualities usually associated with a guide, a coach and a midwife are the ones to look for in a counsellor, therapist or spiritual director.

Guide – in the sense that, though the journey is into our world, we need helpers who know, from their own experience, what such journeys entail – how to begin and how to make sense of what happens. St Ignatius Loyola has this to say to the spiritual director in the introduction to his *Spiritual Exercises*.

> The Director's role is that of helper . . . The retreatant will profit far more from the understanding and love aroused by the grace of God than from the rhetoric or brilliance of me as the retreat Director. When the retreatant is in a time of temptation and desolation, I should be a kind listener and gentle support. I should help to expose the ways in which the powers of evil attempt to block the retreatant's ability to respond to God . . . and I should be careful to present only what is more immediately helpful . . .[8]

Coach – because we need some point of reference outside ourselves. Someone who recognizes our strengths and weaknesses, and who can watch our performance and give us an honest and informative report on it; whose affirmation helps us pick ourselves up, and whose criticism stops us short. Murray Cox, in his book *Structuring the Therapeutic Process,* quotes a patient describing this kind of relationship with a therapist: 'All that there is of me [the patient] is here . . . All you can see of me is all there is. Whereas all of you is not here. It is like American football, part of you is on the side lines waiting to be called on.'[9]

Midwife – as the one who stays with us during our act of creation, of giving birth to some meaning in our lives. For the more we know about ourselves, and particularly about the things which disgust and horrify us, the more chance we have to put ourselves together. As this happens we are bound to feel very vulnerable and in need of reassuring hands which have held 'babies' before, and which neither crush us nor let us fall.

To be a helper requires that we accept the gift and discipline of being helped by someone else. Despite the message of the mystics and the saints, which is mirrored by dynamic psychology, we find it hard to pay attention to our problems and mistakes, our defences and our resistances. Like the Faith and Doubt group described in Chapter 3, we are all for throwing them away and starting all over again. It seems that 'shepherds' have an almost pathological fear of becoming 'sheep', and of learning about their patterns of resistance and defence. Unnoticed, their stresses are redirected to emerge in physical complaints or passed on to their families and their friends, and their own planks appear as specks in the eyes of others. Selves and souls ignored in that way can only give us a hell of a reminder of their existence. Hopefully we will come to see that we deserve a better fate than that. And the church, by encouraging and valuing the active pursuit of self-knowledge amongst its people, will find ways to undo some of the harm that has been done to its servants, its shepherds and its sheep.

> The clergyman has special difficulties in allowing himself adequate opportunities for recreation and personal satisfaction which are so necessary if he is to gain relief from tension . . . In consequence, the minister's marriage, family life, social interests and leisure may all suffer. The minister is thus in a double-bind situation, in which he is bound to experience a sense of failure and guilt . . . So it is critical that he pay close attention to his personal life . . . It is his

vocational responsibility to consciously and deliberately plan opportunities for play, leisure and personal satisfaction; no one else will create such opportunities for him. The responsibility rests with the clergyman.[10]

Would that we were called to account for this and for our vocational responsibility for ourselves, our souls and minds and bodies. In so far as we fail ourselves, not only will we suffer, but we will be a danger to those, like the mentally ill, who elicit our help.

'For the avoidance of error, have someone to advise you, a spiritual father or confessor, a brother of like mind: and make known to him all that happens to you.'[11]

Notes

1. 1 Corinthians 13.12.
2. *The American Journal of Pastoral Psychology,* September 1968, p. 50. Boisen was also the founder of the Clinical Pastoral Education movement in the USA.
3. See Chapter 2, pp. 52–5.
4. H. Eadie, 'The Helping Personality' (*Contact* 49, Summer 1975).
5. See Chapter 3, pp. 70–2.
6. Eadie, op. cit.
7. See Chapter 4, p. 91.
8. St Ignatius Loyola, *The Spiritual Exercises,* translated by D. L. Flemming (The Institute of Jesuit Sources, St Louis, 1978), p. 11; a guide to spiritual directors.
9. M. Cox, *Structuring the Therapeutic Process* (Pergamon Press, 1978), p. 168.
10. Eadie, op. cit.
11. K. Leech, *The Soul Friend,* Sheldon Press, 1977. See page 34 for a quotation from Theophan the Recluse.

Further reading

Bryant, C., *Jung and the Christian Way.* Darton Longman and Todd 1983.
Halmos, P., *The Faith of the Counsellors.* Constable 1965.
Nouwen, H., *The Living Reminder.* Gill and Macmillan, Dublin, 1982.
Williams, H. A., *The True Wilderness.* Constable 1965.

SIX

The Role of Pastoral Counselling

> The greatest trust between man and man is the trust of giving counsel, for in other confidences men commit the parts of their lives – their lands, their goods, their child, their credit, some particular affair – but to such as they make counsellors they commit the whole.[1]

> People become engaged in counselling when a person occupying regularly or temporarily the role of counsellor offers or agrees explicitly to offer time, attention and respect to another person or persons temporarily in the role of client. The task of counselling is to give the client the opportunity to explore, discover and clarify ways of living more resourcefully and toward greater well-being.[2]

Although four centuries separate these two statements, they express what is most fundamental to counselling. It is a work of great trust and commitment, sensitivity and respect which is addressed to the whole of a person's life and not simply to the parts of it. The last twenty years have witnessed a remarkable development in our understanding of counselling, so much so that its place and importance in the life and work of ordinary people, in families, among friends and workmates, and in pastoral care has often been overshadowed by its significance for professional helpers.[3] Lomas warns us of the dangers of this imbalance when writing about psychotherapy, one kind of counselling.

> Once the psychotherapeutic situation is conceived in more differentiated and formal terms than, 'Here is A trying to help B', there is a danger of a gulf developing between the two people which all the training and technique in the world will not bridge. The significant characteristic of the psychotherapeutic situation is that it is, or should be, a place where it is possible to be ordinary in a society that for

> the most part requires people to relate to each other by means of special roles.[4]

On the other hand a great deal has been learnt about the power and effect of relationships, especially those which are entered upon in order to help. Counsellors have learnt, to their cost, that even the most benign and well intentioned interventions can harm rather than help. The quotations above distinguish counselling from such things as the giving of advice and information, guidance and direction, and underline its importance as an activity of mutual trust and exploration. Counsellors are to follow, rather than direct, are not to anticipate their client's needs but to help them find their own way towards greater well-being. In order to develop and improve standards in counselling, and to protect clients from the fallibilities of their helpers, stress has rightly been put upon the counsellor's acquisition of appropriate and professional skills.

In some professions, such as social work, counselling has found a place in their training programmes. This, however, has not been the case in the training of pastors, and the Association for Pastoral Care and Counselling was established to help correct this omission. Blows, writing in the constitutional papers of that association, has this to say about the pastor's needs and the value of counselling:

> The pastor needs help with the intellectual, imaginative and emotional assumptions which structure his perceptions of the human situation around him. He needs to learn to be sensitive to people . . . and to be sufficiently free in himself to be able to respond appropriately to their needs . . . He will need to understand how to use his role, and the authority which it carries, as a creative tool in his work and to recognize both the opportunities and the limitations it presents. He will need to know about human growth and development as it is described by the behavioural sciences and something of the ways in which this growth can be helped and hindered. He will need, finally, to be able to relate what he learns to his understanding of the Christian tradition in such a way that both are challenged and illuminated by each other.[5]

To learn and develop such expertise, and remain one's self requires an artist's dedication and discipline, the aim being to integrate oneself with one's art, so as to express the former more truthfully and more fully through the other. Just as artists have to harness their natural abilities by long and laborious practice, so too pastors have to serve an apprenticeship. Learning to counsel is one aspect of that apprenticeship. For some it will become their major or only work, for the majority it can inform and enlighten every aspect of pastoral care. The roots of contemporary counselling stretch in many directions and touch a number of other disciplines, but it is psychology, both dynamic and behavioural, which has contributed most to the theory and practice of counselling.

Dynamic or analytic psychology has plumbed the depths of the mystery which St Paul describes in such anguished terms in his letter to the Romans: 'For I do not do the good I want, but the evil I do not want is what I do.'[6] Freud and his followers used the concept of the unconscious to help us observe and then make sense of our behaviour. In their view we are the inhabitants of an unconscious and internal world, no less important than the external one of which we are conscious. Indeed it is the former which affects us most. The habits we learn, the emotions we exhibit, the feelings we express or reject, the beliefs we espouse, the attitudes we hold and condemn, for the most part all are determined by the energy of that unconscious and internal world. A world peopled by those most significant to us, our parents with whom we first related and failed to relate, our siblings and others closest to us in those earliest and most formative years.

According to dynamic psychology, we put down an internal template upon our contemporary experience. In our present relationships, we find uncanny reminders of how we were with our parents; our methods of coping and living reflect how we learnt or failed to learn from them. We hear ourselves repeating their affirmations and accusations, and behaving towards ourselves just as they did. What is more, we imagine our contemporary relationships to be the same. We expect others to treat us just as we have always been treated. All of this is mostly unconscious to us, because we need to defend ourselves against such a frightening world. Among the many defences which Freud identified, projection is one often used by religious people. We find it hard, if not impossible to acknowledge feelings of anger and rage, desire and lust. We disown them by projecting them onto others, whom we identify as bad and faithless, and deserving our condemnation.

Counsellors have drawn heavily upon these theories in order to make sense of the confusing behaviour of their clients. David and his counsellor, in Chapter 4, illustrate how a counsellor and client can work together to reveal the power of the client's unconscious. They bring his internal world slowly forward out of its prison and into the light, where it can be examined and understood, and ultimately resolved and reordered.[7] Equally, clients can reclaim what they have projected, by owning and accepting in themselves what they hate or fear in others.

Pastors, who are also counsellors, need to be aware of their special significance for their clients. Their vocation, to bear others' burdens, draws them to share in, and so to carry other people's hopes and fears, distress and happiness. The conversations and stories in Part One illustrated how pastoral counselling can help people to bear and express their strongest feelings, and how the pastor comes to weep with those who weep and rejoice with those who rejoice. The burden of this, is, of course, considerable. Pastors need help to recognize what they carry for others, lest they believe that what they feel is only to do with them personally. In Chapter 2 Emma's chaplain felt the weight of her sense of failure as though it was his own. Just as people condemn in others what they can not face in themselves, so they value in some what they can not believe about themselves. Joan tells her chaplain: 'Any human kindness is good, but kindness based on religion is better.'[8] Goodness projected on to pastors can be admired. ('They can do no wrong') or feared ('Someone so good must judge me because I'm not so good'). The consequences of these projections are legion, and can so easily confuse and delude helpers and helped. In psychoanalysis and psychotherapy the unconscious is explored directly in a very specific and often lengthy therapeutic relationship. This is not usually the case with counselling or with pastoral work in general, but pastors and counsellors are greatly helped if they are aware of the unconscious forces which are inevitably active in their work. In this way dynamic psychology makes a unique contribution to the counselling movement, and it is the reason why many counsellors and pastors turn to psychotherapists for help and supervision.

Behavioural psychology has given counselling the insights of learning and cognitive theory, and has underlined the value of simply studying what can be observed of human behaviour. Psychologists of this school persistently seek better ways to measure human behaviour and to identify the links between cause and effect. They observe how the forces of reward and punishment determine people's growth and development and how, by the introduction of different stimuli, that growth and development is modified and changed. From their observations they have produced pragmatic learning programmes to help people overcome particular problems and to change unwanted and incapacitating patterns of behaviour.[9]

This approach has influenced counsellors to try and evaluate their work on similar lines. There are of course enormous problems to the research of anything so variable and sensitive as counselling, but attempts have been made to identify what it is that counsellors do — what helps and what it is that can harm. The books listed at the end of this chapter provide more information about the history and development of counselling. Egan's book is representative of the fruits of the evaluative approach mentioned above. The books by Jacobs and Kennedy illustrate a combination of approaches for those learning about counselling. Brown and Pedder write about counselling from a psychotherapeutic foundation, and Proctor reviews a range of current counselling theories and methods.

As counselling forms only one part of the ministry of most pastors, clerical and lay, the insights and practice of specialized counselling have to be adapted for their work of pastoral care and more limited pastoral counselling. So I will now concentrate upon that adaption, upon what experience reveals and research supports as the essential prerequisites of any counselling relationship. Attention to these essentials is the best way to begin counselling with anyone in any setting, and especially with those made vulnerable by the handicap of 'madness' of whatever kind.

Qualities of effective counselling

The essentials of the counselling relationship were first objectively researched by Truax and Carkhuff.[10] Though they themselves were trained in Rogerian or non-directive therapy, they set out to investigate a wide variety of counselling methods, and from their work they identified the following characteristics as most helpful irrespective of the individual practitioner's philosophy or method. In the same way as ecclesiastical diagnosticians look for the so-called 'marks' of the effective church, they noted the 'marks' or qualities of effective counselling. Their research among helpers of all kinds – teachers, parents, counsellors, community and race relations workers – first revealed three qualities; then in further work they and others identified six qualities in all. They then confirmed their research by demonstrating the value of training helpers to recognize and develop these qualities in their work.

The first three – empathy, respect and concreteness – are the more passive and responsive qualities. They are essential to all counselling and are particularly important in the initial stages. Genuineness, confrontation and immediacy are the later qualities which help clients move from support and understanding towards insight and change.

Empathy

> He is looking at me. He don't say nothing, just looks at me with them queer eyes of his that makes folk talk. I always say it ain't never been what he done, so much, or said or anything, so much as how he looks at you. It's like he had got into the inside of you someway. Like somehow you was looking at yourself and your doing outer his eyes.[11]

I remember one of my sons going to help his young cousin who had fallen over and hurt herself. He tried to pick her up, but she stayed where she was and cried all the more. Then her brother came and sat down with her, he held her hand and waited until she was ready to get up by herself. Empathy is the ability to get inside another person, to try and think their thoughts and feel their feelings, to look out through their eyes, and to convey as accurately as one can the sense of being with them – not behind them, misunderstanding or misreading their experience, and not ahead of them as my son was, but with them where they are and in their way.

PAM: I was so upset, my husband went to see the manager, and he assured him that I had nothing to do with it. My husband keeps telling me that I'm imagining it, and that it is all in my mind. But I know these things happen, people do talk about me. Do you think I imagine it all?

MINISTER: It all seems very real to you, Pam, and I can understand that you are very distressed.[12]

We are often defeated in our attempts to be empathetic, because sitting where others sit is often costly and painful. We stagger under the weight of their feelings and our own emotional wounds are reopened and infected. Either we draw back from the closeness which empathy requires, or we fear that our presence so near to what is painful will reinforce its destructive quality and make things worse, and if we fail to stem our fears, our being there may add to their force. We fear listening to the delusions of the mentally ill, in case we imprison them further in their irrational world.

Such fears are to be taken seriously, and are best managed with the help of colleagues to show us how and where they have hindered our empathy. Empathy is learnt by practice and by imagining what it is like to be this other person: how it sounds to speak their words, with their tone and affect, what it is like to sit in the way they sit, and to imagine the world through their eyes. And if we can act and speak like them in a role-play with a colleague, we get a first-hand sense of how they may experience others.

> I suspect that we, in our church, don't always take trouble enough entering the experience of others. We're ready to help physical suffering, and we're ready to make allowances for emotional distress. But we won't always go the extra mile to achieve imaginative understanding. There's a phrase that's used casually – 'I'm with you' – meaning something's understood. Those people who feel set apart in their unhappiness are longing to hear it, but it will only ring true if we've troubled to make the journey all the way.[13]

Respect

> Jesus looked up and said to him, 'Zacchaeus, make haste and come down; for I must stay at your house today.[14]

Respect for one's self, like love for one's self is not easy, especially at those times when people's problems have brought them to the point of seeking help. They come humiliated and distrustful, and now with the additional weight of being a burden to someone else. 'I am sorry to take your time and lay my troubles upon you,' is a common way for people to begin. At that moment they need to be respected and to meet someone who understands their disrespect for themselves and their fear of being a burden. It is neither helpful nor respectful to tell them they are no trouble. It is much better to acknowledge the courage they found, albeit unconsciously, in coming for help. The counsellor who shows respect for a client's courage and honesty will stimulate the kind of trust which will help them begin to change. 'Loving the sinner and not the sin,' dubious catch-phrase though it is, has some value in this context. Our respect has to be non-judgemental, and non-possessive. It must not depend upon the client pleasing us, taking our advice, or getting better. We have to respect them whatever they say or do. Sarah told the chaplain that she feared infecting him with her 'badness'. He said that he did not experience her like that and went on, 'You do not frighten me. I want to come and see you however you are.'[15]

Counsellors find it difficult to show respect when they are upset by what people tell them. Although they may cultivate a mask of unshockability, their feelings are not so easily hidden, and will affect their response in any case. Furthermore, counsellors are often anxious that their apparent acceptance of the frightening and distasteful things which clients say and do, will reinforce these in the client. Respecting a client can feel like condoning their behaviour. It is a narrow line to tread, but in showing acceptance for the worst in people, counsellors create an atmosphere in which everything, good and bad, hopeful and desperate, can be brought out into the light. Hate, envy, despair and disgust do not go away by being ignored or condemned. If, however, they are acknowledged, then counsellor and counselled have the chance to understand what they represent, and to find a more creative and healthy way of expressing their energy and meaning.

'But the tax collector, standing far off, would not even lift up his eyes to heaven, but beat his breast, saying, "God be merciful to me, a sinner". I tell you, this man went down to his house justified.'[16] There is only one way to learn respect for others and that is to develop a respect for the whole of ourselves, for what we dislike and usually reject about ourselves as much as what we value and admire. The Faith and Doubt discussion group, described in Chapter 3, illustrates both the value and the difficulty of grasping and holding this quality.

Concreteness

> And as Jesus was setting out on his journey, a man ran up and knelt before him, and asked him, 'Good Teacher, what must I do to inherit eternal life?' . . . And Jesus looking upon him loved him, and said to him, 'You lack one thing; go, sell what you have, and give to the poor, and you will have treasure in heaven; and come, follow me.'[17]

'Eternal life', important though it is, is frustratingly and unhelpfully vague, just as are the problems and needs which lead people to seek help. Misery, fear and anxiety are often general states about which it is difficult to be specific. So often they make us feel like a rudderless boat adrift in an ocean of troubles. Counsellors who encourage clients to move gradually from the general to the specific help the most. Jesus helped the young man discover that his quest for eternal life was matched by a love of riches. So often it is the case that a generalized longing or need for relief obscures a quite specific vulnerability. It is often a long road from one to the other but, once started, ground can be quickly made up. Much of the work of behavioural psychologists and therapists revolves around helping clients make their problems more concrete and so more manageable. A specific problem or need can then be tackled step by step, and success at each stage is the basis for the next step to be taken.

CHAPLAIN: What prevents you launching out?

DAVID: Yes, what am I frightened of? . . . That really is

strange. I've not thought of that before. I'm frightened of showing myself. Yes, of being exposed. It reminds me of being at school, little and spotty and bullied, as though that's how I would be seen.[18]

It is difficult to be concrete especially in the early stages of counselling. Specific difficulties appear inconsequential beside the huge problems which overwhelm people, and counsellors are easily put off by the pessimism and disillusionment of their clients. Joan and Emma, in Chapter 2, had something of this effect upon their chaplains. At other times a client's inability to be definite will prompt the counsellor into being concrete instead, and filling the vacuum by guess work, as Edward's chaplain did. Counsellors need to be patient and to await their client's readiness to move from the general to the specific. The more carefully they listen and observe, the more accurately they will identify the clues dropped by their clients. A change of tone in their voice, a different facial expression will often be the signs of a specific feeling which is struggling into the client's consciousness. Counsellors can practise being concrete with themselves by defining and clarifying their own feelings as accurately as they can, and noting the specific things or events which give rise to those feelings.

These first three qualities are responsive. They show that counsellors aim to understand their clients, from the client's point of view. Their accurate empathy enables them to enter the client's world, their respect to demonstrate that this intrusion is for their client's sake, and their concreteness is evidence of their willingness to confront the roots of a client's distress. A relationship which offers these qualities is the one most likely to help people enter, explore and make sense of their inner and unconscious world. And yet it is not easy for either counsellor or client to trust in these qualities as that exploration gets underway. The illustrations in Chapter 2 show just how hard it is for pastors to avoid being overrun by their own anxieties and leading or diverting their clients. At the same time, clients themselves often demonstrate a resilience and readiness to help their counsellors return to the task in hand. In that sense it is our clients who will, over time, teach us the most about how to offer these qualities.

Once the relationship has been established by the appropriate use of these responsive qualities, then it is possible for counsellors to become more active in their helping, although the relative emotional and personal strength of the client must be the determining factor at this point. For instance, a person in great distress or crisis, who has been recently bereaved, or someone undergoing a psychotic crisis, like Edward or Sarah in Chapter 2, is best served by the continued offering of the qualities already mentioned, particularly empathy and respect. At such times the counsellor's patient and reassuring presence is the most powerful agent in helping people gain greater control of themselves and their emotions. This is generally called 'supportive counselling' and is often the most demanding. As supportive counsellors we are drawn into the midst of someone else's suffering and their pain begins to invade us. Furthermore, our presence becomes so important that more and more of our time and attention is demanded. We feel crushed by the magnitude of another's distress and drained of all our resources. 'And Jesus, perceiving in himself that power had gone forth from him, immediately turned about in the crowd, and said, "Who touched my garments?"'[19] It is hardly surprising, therefore, that counsellors should want to extricate themselves from this kind of relationship, by offering interpretations or demanding some movement of their client. A better alternative is for them to set reasonable limits upon the relationship, of time and attention, so that what they offer is genuine and not half-hearted. At the same time they should provide themselves with the support of colleagues or a supervisor to help them hang on to the limits they have set.

However, for many clients the establishment of a trusting and accepting relationship is only the first stage, and they and their counsellor must look for more active involvement with one another if more is to be got from their counselling. Three more qualities, or 'marks', are associated with this second phase.

Genuineness

> And they were astonished at his teaching, for he taught them as one who had authority, and not as the scribes.[20]

The quality that psychiatric patients most often admire in those new to the helping professions is their genuineness, unaffected as it is at that stage by their professional role. For instance, in Chapter 2, the chaplain ends her conversation with Joan by thanking her for the help she has been. Joan is surprised and asks how she has helped. 'Well, I am trying to learn how best to bring help to people in hospital. Now, you started a conversation with me about God and faith, and that gave me the chance to talk to you about these matters, and to think hard how to answer the questions you raised, how to help you, if possible. I don't think I've done very well, but still, I apreciate the chance you have given me to talk to you.'[21]

Genuineness is best conveyed by counsellors being honest and open about themselves. That does not mean giving their views or showing their feelings indiscriminately, but rather by being direct and undefended. Counsellors should not pretend they understand when they do not, that they have answers when they have not, or that they were listening when, for a moment, they were distracted. Pretence, of course, can save us from discomfort and disapproval, but this will be at the expense of the trust which genuineness can cement. Genuineness is best learnt by monitoring our own responses. For usually we are least ourselves when our anxieties are touched. If we know and recognize the subjects or feelings which most affect us, we can begin to anticipate when we are likely to retreat behind the safety of our special role, to play 'priest' or 'counsellor'. Being honest with ourselves and our clients about such manoeuvres when we have fallen into them, is the best place to begin. Then we create an atmosphere in which mistakes are as acceptable as they are inevitable.

Confrontation

> When Jesus saw him and knew that he had been lying there a long time, he said to him, 'Do you want to be healed?' The sick man answered, 'Sir, I have no man to put me into the pool when the water is troubled, and while I am going another steps down before me.' Jesus said to him, 'Rise, take up your pallet, and walk.'[22]

Confrontation is not the easiest of qualities to master effectively. In a way it is the reverse side of empathy. Through confrontation, counsellors invite their clients to look at themselves through the counsellor's eyes, to see how they appear not from within themselves but more objectively. Counsellors confront their clients when they see or hear something inconsistent. What a client says may appear to be in direct conflict with the way they act, or they may talk about some traumatic event without showing any emotion. It is best if counsellors simply express the way that they see such things and invite their clients to speculate with them about what this may mean. It is important to confront with interest and curiosity, rather than judgement or criticism, so that clients are helped to explore further rather than to justify or explain. Confrontation, to be effective, requires a high degree of trust, and when it is built upon empathy and respect in the earlier stages of counselling, it is a potent tool in beginning to initiate change.

The story of Jesus and the woman at the well in St John's Gospel is a remarkable study of the effective use of confrontation within a relationship. Jesus helps the woman reveal her need only after she has served his need, by drawing him some water. He supports her as she tries to piece together what has happened in her life, and to her faith, and how her experience of him has enlarged her vision. 'So the woman left her water jar, and went away into the city, and said to the people, 'Come, see a man who told me all that I ever did. Can this be the Christ?'[23]

Tell 'the truth in love', the author of the Epistle to the Ephesians advises his readers, and so too counsellors are well advised to take special care of their clients' reactions to confrontation, the hurt and pain they can feel. Clients are unlikely to be grateful, they may ignore or return the counsellor's gift with a sample of their own confrontation about insensitive helpers. This illustrates the major difficulty of confrontation. We fail to confront when we should, because we fear the consequences. If we can overcome that fear, perhaps with the help of a colleague, to rehearse what we want to say, then the feelings engendered by the confrontation are likely to work for, rather than against, us and our counselling.

'I hated you for calling me arrogant, or rather getting me to call myself arrogant. I hate that about myself. I feel so humiliated and before your eyes, and yet not your eyes, it was me looking at myself through your eyes and condemning myself as I always do.' This is an example of a patient's reaction to a chaplain's confrontation.

Immediacy

> When they had finished breakfast, Jesus said to Simon Peter, 'Simon, son of John, do you love me more than these?' He said to him, 'Yes, Lord; you know that I love you.' He said to him, 'Feed my lambs.'[24]

More often than not people's problems and difficulties involve their relationships. Past experiences have left scars, which today's events reopen. Clients come to repair what still hurts, and to learn how to manage better what they always get wrong. In counselling they make yet another relationship, which is open to being a repetition of past failures and a place for the re-enactment of at least some of the conflicts, hopes and fears of previous relationships. Counsellors come to realize why their clients elicit such anger or panic in others, because that is how they begin to feel towards them. When what we offer or say fails to help our clients their feelings towards us change, deference is replaced by resistance, placation by argument. As counselling develops, it is possible to talk about what is happening between counsellor and client, and to demonstrate how similar or different this is to the client's other relationships. In Chapter 4, for instance, David often experienced the counsellor both as a positive force for good, someone who could really help him, but also as someone who let him down by failing to say or do the things which would have communicated his 'standing by' David. This reminded David of his feelings for his father.

There are many illustrations in the Gospels of how sensitive Jesus was to the hidden and unspoken reactions which his behaviour caused in others; he anticipated and drew out from them the things which preoccupied them. Counsellors need to be alert to the unconscious reactions which their efforts provoke in their clients, in order to bring them to the surface and face them openly. Often painful and difficult disclosures will leave clients feeling vulnerable for having said too much, and they will leave an interview fearing the counsellor's judgement of them. At such moments it is particularly helpful if that fear is acknowledged by the counsellor saying something like this: 'I sense that you feel you have said more than you wanted to, you would like to retract it, but you can't and so you seem to be judging yourself or perhaps imagining that I might be.'

Immediacy is an important quality for it involves addressing the counselling relationship itself, in order to influence it while it happens. Most people in times of distress feel at the mercy of the destructiveness of their ways of relating, so much so that they fear they will never manage them any better. Relating to a counsellor gives the client the chance to experiment, to fail and to try again without fear of being rejected.

These then are the marks and qualities of effective counselling. Clients who find these qualities in their counsellors are likely to understand and accept themselves better, and to be able to make the changes in themselves which they want. They will experience sufficient security to take themselves and their disturbing unconscious inner worlds seriously. They will be able to explore their behaviour more freely and to find within themselves gifts and resources of which they were unaware.

Training

In the second chapter, it was suggested that there is a significant difference between a counselling conversation and an ordinary one, and yet the six qualities described in this chapter are essentially human qualities. All of us possess them to a greater or lesser extent. This is because counselling seeks to apply what is natural and human in a specific way for a specific end. Obviously some people are better suited to applying their humanity in this way than others. But most of us can learn to develop our latent abilities as helpers, to be more empathetic and more respectful, etc., and initial training in counselling aims to do just that. More and more of the helping professions now require some training of this kind for their workers, and it is likely to become more mandatory for pastors.

Learning to counsel involves a number of things. Counsellors need to grow in self-understanding, to recognize and appreciate, for instance, which of the counselling qualities they are best and worst at. They need, too, to understand their own patterns of relating and why it is they are drawn to be helpers and counsellors. It is difficult, if not impossible, to counsel others effectively if one has never experienced the value of counselling for one's self. Once would-be counsellors have achieved a reasonable basis of self-knowledge, then it is possible for them to move on to practise and make their own the qualities stressed in this chapter. Many introductory counselling courses or counselling-skills courses emphasize training of this kind. Students are taught the qualities or skills, one by one, and with the help of audio and video aids, they can practise using them with one another. The next step in learning is one of application. Counsellors need to try themselves out, to use the responses they have learnt in training in their work of helping. This should always be accompanied by supervision (see below), which some courses will automatically provide. When it is not provided, counsellors should find their own supervision. The British Association for Counselling and its pastoral division, the Association for Pastoral Care and Counselling have the fullest information about counselling courses.[25]

Supervision

'Supervision' is a new word to most pastors, and yet it must have its origin in the Church's work of pastoral care. Bishops and presbyters have always been responsible for the oversight and care of others. In Chapter 5, it was made clear how valuable it is for a pastor to have a 'soul friend' or 'counsellor'. It is equally important, for those of us who care for others, not to care alone or in isolation. Counsellors who are supported by supervision are able to involve themselves more freely and effectively in their work with clients. In supervision they can reflect on what they have done and said, with concerned and critical colleagues whose distance from their work provides a 'transcendent' element to match the 'incarnate' one which they bring. At first most people find supervision difficult. We are anxious about being criticized by an expert, and we have a quite proper concern for the confidentiality of our work. However, if we persevere, it is quickly apparent how supervision can enhance our counselling. Supervision is not for supervisors to demonstrate their brilliance or to do the counselling at one remove, but to enable counsellors to reflect upon their work, to understand it and their clients better and to prepare themselves for the next step. The supervisor's comments in Chapter 2, illustrate how supervision is done and what it achieves.

Conclusion

Sometimes it may seem that the philosophies and assumptions which underlie counselling are at variance with those that inspire both psychiatry and religion.

Psychiatry

Psychiatry as a part of medicine often appears to foster inequality in the relationship between helper and helped. The latter has an illness which the former will treat and endeavour to cure, and the medical model assumes that helpers will have the necessary skill and knowledge and the helped sufficient patience and trust. Slowly however, psychiatry is discovering that such a relationship can create an impasse which is of little use to either, and leads inevitably to the revolving door syndrome of mental institutions. Psychiatry is beginning to cast envious eyes upon the counselling movement, as a way of helping and treating which induces less dependence and more responsibility in its clients. Gosling expresses this change of perspective when writing about the Richmond Fellowship, an organization whose interests span psychiatry, counselling and religion.

> In the stance of infantile dependency which normally dominates welfare organizations [the Church as well?] there is an assumption, that to be strong or 'grown up' is the aim of everyone . . . In welfare operations the workers offer goods and services that will supplement what the client

> already has to an inadequate extent . . . A negotiating stance, however, implies an exchange of goods and services, in which each can go away considering himself the richer. The relationship in no way implies that it is the aim of one member of the pair to become like the other.[26]

Counsellors now speak of the 'equal but asymmetrical' nature of their work, in order to define the equal in value but different in role aspects of their own and their client's positions. All too often these roles can only be understood by people as hierarchical. Clients need to experience their own worth, and also the value to them of counselling, in some quite tangible way. For instance payment of fees for counselling can provide a basis for clients to receive and use what is valuable to them in the counsellor's role. The apparently free service of both National Health Service psychiatry and the Church (of course it is not really free) can so obscure as to render impotent the real value of counselling to helper and helped. This is sadly reflected in some of the recent debate about the proposed move in psychiatry from hospital to community care. At recent meetings to discuss the transference of resources from one to the other, it is often recognized that resistance to such change would inevitably come from those whose livelihood depends upon institutions, and who are not easily or happily relocated in the community. Helper and helped, weak and strong will unite in their dependency to protect themselves from such unwelcome change. Counselling is often acceptable as a means of getting individuals back into their proper place, but is not so welcome when it subverts a secure but unhealthy *status quo.*

Religion

Religious people are unsure of counselling for similar reasons. They, too, are more accustomed to a dependent and hierarchical stance; the non-directiveness and lack of judgement in counselling does not commend itself to most religiously committed people. This conflict of assumptions is real, but it rests upon a superficial understanding of both religion and counselling. Campbell illustrates clearly how counselling has uncovered, and then sometimes overcompensated for the inadequacies of much pastoral care.[27] He then goes on to point out how the mutuality of carer and cared for is at the heart of what the Bible means by pastoral care.

It is true that the counselling movement has helped us develop emotionally much more than ethically. Here surely is an area where pastoral counselling is of the greatest importance. What is clear is that counselling stands for the belief stated at the beginning of this chapter: that individuals have the capacity to understand themselves, to solve their own problems, to make their own decisions and to act upon them. It also believes that individuals will be helped to do this by counsellors who are neither better nor worse than their clients, but who, for the purpose of counselling, will act in a different role. Counsellors allow clients to depend upon them for one thing only, their skill in helping clients help themselves. This principle is as important for an individual's beliefs and conduct as it is for their emotions and their thoughts.

> The message for the counsellor and the teacher [for the pastor too] is no easy one. Nobody can give meaning to someone else, and the counsellor who tries to offer meaning to his client, or the teacher who attempts to teach moral principles, are both equally doomed to failure. The moral sense cannot be taught or imposed: it can only be discovered . . . The counsellor and the teacher faced by such a task have no alternative but to demonstrate their own personal commitment to search for truth and meaning.[28]

In Chapter 2, Joan spelt this out to the chaplain who had just conveyed serious doubts about her ability to help communicate the faith. Joan said, 'Oh, but you have helped me. You have brought me *your* faith, and I can rest on that, even if I have none of my own.'[29] The truth is that those who have their own faith, be that a faith in God, or in people, are able to offer something quite unique to others. A faith with flesh for them to lean upon, while they search for their own faith. Where as those who have *a* faith or *the* faith, but not yet their own faith, are often so preoccupied with passing it on to others, that it is lost to everyone. Words and ideas fly all over the place, and without the flesh of ownership they have no substance.

Notes

1. R. Bacon, *The Essays (1597–1625),* Routledge, 1895.
2. British Association for Counselling, *The Definition of Counselling,* 1980.
3. P. Halmos, *The Faith of the Counsellors,* Constable, 1978.
4. P. Lomas, *True and False Experience,* (Allen Lane, 1973), p. 19.
5. D. Blows, *The Association for Pastoral Care and Counselling,* Constitutional Papers, 1973.
6. Romans 7.19.
7. See Chapter 4, pp. 75–82.
8. See Chapter 2, 'Emma', pp. 30–9.
   See Chapter 2, 'Joan', pp. 14–29.
9. See Chapter 7, pp. 132–3.
10. C. B. Truax, and R. R. Carkhuff, *Towards Effective Counselling and Psychotherapy,* Aldine, Chicago, 1965. See also R. R. Carkhuff, *The Development of Human Resources,* Holt, Reinhart and Winston, 1971.
11. W. Faulkner, *As I Lay Dying,* Penguin, 1963.
12. See Chapter 2, pp. 10–13.
13. R. Runcie, *Canterbury Diocese Newservice,* January 1983.
14. Luke 19.5.
15. See Chapter 2, p. 60.
16. Luke 18. 13–14.
17. Mark 10. 17–21.
18. See Chapter 4, p. 81.
19. Mark 5.30.
20. Mark 1.22.
21. See Chapter 2, p. 26.
22. John 5.6.
23. John 4.29. See also L. Marteau, *Words of Counsel* (Shand, 1978), pp. 84ff.
24. John 21.15.
25. See Useful Addresses page.
26. R. Gosling, *The Richmond Fellowship, Annual Report 1979–80,* pp. 23–31.
27. A. Campbell, *The Rediscovery of Pastoral Care,* Darton Longman and Todd, 1981.
28. B. Thorne, 'In Search of Value and Meaning' (*Theology*, SPCK, January 1979), pp. 16–24.
29. See Chapter 2, p. 28.

Further Reading

Brown, D. and Pedder, J., *Introduction to Psychotherapy.* Tavistock 1979.
Clinebell, H., *Basic Type of Pastoral Counselling.* Abingdon, Nashville, 1966.
Egan, G., *The Skilled Helper.* Brooks Cole, California, 1975.
Jacobs, M., *Still Small Voice.* SPCK 1982.
Kennedy, E., *On Becoming a Counsellor.* Gill and Macmillan, Dublin, 1977.
Proctor, B., *Counselling Shop.* Deutsch 1978.

SEVEN

Psychiatry and Mental Illness

> Many of them said, 'He has a demon, and he is mad; why listen to him?'[1]

> Anyone who has reflected on the many definitions of health and of mental health in particular, will, I think, conclude that there is no consensus, and he will see that when moral or social values are invoked there are scarcely any limits to the behaviour which might be called morbid.[2]

The phenomena that are associated with madness, namely the disturbances and disorders which affect a person's mind and behaviour, have a long and confusing history, during which time recognition of the signs and symptoms has remained remarkably consistent. Determination of causes and their significance, resolution and cure is still shrouded in considerable mystery. So much so that the very notion of 'madness' being an illness at all, has undergone an unprecedented attack in the last twenty years.[3]

Succeeding generations have used different languages and hypotheses, some more elaborate than others, to describe and explain 'madness'. For some the concern has been to isolate and segregate the phenomena of insanity, either by exorcising the spirit or devil from the sufferers, or by placing the insane themselves out of harm's way in a secure asylum. Others have been fascinated by the irrational itself, regarding the mad as inspired, and in touch with a reality more profound than that afforded the rest of us. In turn the mad have been treated and cared for, imprisoned and tortured, ridiculed and admired. All the major institutions of our society, legal and religious, medical and political, have contributed both to the care and to the abuse of the insane. Present-day attitudes among those who suffer and those who treat, and among people in general, reflect this confused history, namely the recognition and acknowledgement of the observable facts, and a baffling uncertainty about causes and cures. There is only a small harvest from years of study and research, which goes some way to explain the three most obvious features of mental illness and psychiatry today.

First the stigma of 'madness', which attaches itself to the mentally ill and their families, and causes others to see them as different. For instance, Pam in Chapter 2 was struggling with her fears about the stigma of madness.[4]

Secondly, the faith, at times fanatical, which helper and helped place in one method or approach. As if the scarcity of effective treatments accentuated the urgency to find and then believe in, a single cure to cure all ills. In the last thirty years, there have been many developments in medical treatments, and a succession of new therapies. Though each one is heralded as near miraculous in its healing potential, time reveals each to be effective with a few problems of a few people.

Thirdly, the desperate picture of diminishing resources chasing ever-growing needs, which the following quotation, appearing in a report of the Royal College of Psychiatrists,[5] illustrates so clearly:

> The average standard of psychiatric practice in Britain is abysmally low. Psychiatrists themselves are sometimes reluctant to make this admission but the evidence is overwhelming. In an average mental hospital, a long-stay patient is likely to see a doctor for only ten minutes or so every three months. Even a recently admitted patient is seen by a doctor on average for twenty minutes each week. The tenuous contact between the psychiatrist and his patient is reflected in the case-notes which are often almost uninformative. Scandals about the ill-treatment of patients in mental hospitals, including those of relatively good reputation, occur with monotonous regularity.[6]

In the last ten years little has happened to alter this picture. If anything should stir the pastor's sense of compassion, it is the sadness and hopelessness which so often engulf the mentally ill, and all who have to do with them, be they their relatives or their helpers. Would that a corporate anger at their lot stirred the churches and similar bodies within society to greater understanding and action. The recent attacks on the concept of mental illness and the practices of the mental health professions, express the sense of frustration which drives people to seek a way out of this paralysis. In Italy, for instance, frustration has provided the energy for a quiet revolution, including the closure of mental hospitals, and the giving over of care to the community.[7] Less ambitious experiments have been tried and are planned in our health service – and recently the Department of Health and Social Security, MIND and the Richmond Fellowship have all produced documents about the possibilities and problems of community care.[8] They go further than the reiteration of pious hopes, addressing the nature of the malaise and looking for ways to overcome institutional and social resistance to change.

This then is an important time in which to understand what is happening to the mentally ill, to recognize the inadequacies and inconsistencies of what is offered to them, and to anticipate the direction in which future services may best be developed. This requires some grasp of the approaches to, and the theories and ideologies about 'madness', which typify the major psychiatric schools of thought, and are sometimes described as the different models of 'madness'.

The models of 'madness'

Listen to any group of people talking about insanity and before long their view upon it will be revealed. For some it is illness, for others, badness, the devil or the state of the economy. Our models of 'madness', imprecise and conflicting as they are, speak eloquently, both of its mystery and of our urgent need to contain and understand that mystery. Like many other formulations of the inherently mysterious, the models are more obvious for their limitations than they are for their completeness. And yet they are all we have to inform the attitudes we hold, the care and the counsel we give.

The medical or illness model

This model assumes that the phenomena of madness, the

signs and symptoms experienced by the sufferers, and observed by those close to them, are caused by a physical or chemical imbalance, disturbance or disorder to the central nervous system. As other illnesses attack the major organs of the body, so mental illness attacks the brain. Following the patterns tried and tested with physical illnesses, the physicians (psychiatrists) concentrate their attention upon the accurate recognition of the signs and symptoms in order to diagnose the mental illness. As with much else in medicine, the development of this model has depended upon the scientific method of trial and error – the formulation of hypotheses, followed by a systematic and painstaking search for adequate evidence to prove or disprove their efficacy. For some illnesses the connection between the symptoms and an objectively identifiable organic disorder has been established. That is to say, the malfunction or deterioration within the brain is observable, as for instance was the case with Harry in Chapter 3, who suffered from senile dementia. Mental handicap and epilepsy are other organic disorders.

For the majority of conditions, however, this is not the case. The link, if there is one, between the symptoms and some organic or chemical disorder, is yet to be found. At best it is a matter of relative association, which extensive research makes more or less probable. Those committed to the medical model continue to search, as do their colleagues in physical medicine, for the causes, for the connections between symptoms and some demonstrable deficiency or disturbance, and for 'cures' which, if effective, will imply a connection as yet unproved. There has been considerable progress in medical and drug treatments over the last twenty years, so much so that many of those who were once totally incapacitated by their illnesses, are now able to lead more normal lives.

Similar symptom alleviation has also come from the practice of some physical treatments. Electro-convulsive therapy (ECT), the passing of a small electric current through a patient's brain in order to induce a fit similar to that of an epileptic fit, is a treatment which has helped sufferers from depression, who did not respond to other medical treatment. Although still used in some places, there is no evidence to support the practice of psychosurgery (leucotomy and lobotomy). Popular and professional concern about the irreversible nature of physical treatments, such as ECT and psychosurgery, and the side effects of medical treatments, has been balanced by a belief in, and experience of, their efficacy. Proponents of both views marshall similar kinds and quantities of evidence to support their case. Objective data is in short supply,[9] and this highlights the problem central to the medical model.

Accurate diagnosis of mental illness is extremely difficult, depending as it often does upon the subjective experience, both of sufferers and of those who observe their suffering. Establishing links between treatments and illnesses is equally hazardous, given the mysterious nature of the illnesses and our incomplete knowledge of how treatment, medical or physical, actually works. Proceeding by way of relative association (e.g. sufferers from this illness generally get better with this treatment) is an acceptable way to proceed in the absence of anything better, so long as the treatment has no other detrimental effects. It is well known that the irreversible factors in physical treatments and the side effects of medical treatments can affect sufferers for better or for worse. It is less clear, before the administration of treatment, which it is to be. If you do not treat, you will never know if a sufferer has been denied reasonable alleviation from his illness. If you do treat, you run the risk of making him better or worse.

As the major model for 'madness', the medical one attracts considerable attention and criticism. Is the alleviation of suffering important for its own sake, or is it better to endure the pain in order to discover and understand its cause? At both extremes mental health professionals join the popular prophets in becoming evangelists or cynics. The former pursue their method of treatment with much zeal, some scientific evidence and anecdotal testimonies to their success. The latter question the whole basis of such certainties, and demand that the medical model itself be subjected to closer and more critical scrutiny. The majority of sufferers and carers find themselves in the grey middle ground between these extremes. They know that whatever may be possible in an ideal world, they have to confront the most bewildering problems with few resources, and little expertise.[10]

The psychodynamic model

This model locates the causes of 'madness' not in some material, physical or chemical imbalance, but in the personality or psyche of the sufferer – that is, in an 'internal world' of the individual, metaphorical and yet very real. It is a world formed out of a person's earliest experiences from the time of their birth and perhaps earlier, that is, within the womb. Their personalities, their strengths and weaknesses have been shaped and fashioned through the relationship with their parents. All of this is deeply buried within us in what Freud[11] described as the unconscious. This is the motivator and manager of behaviour, for the most part unavailable to consciousness, but identifiable in dreams, slips of the tongue and inconsistencies of thought and action.

According to this model, all of us are affected by our beginnings: by our experience of birth, of being fed and loved, nursed and ignored; and by the traumas we negotiated or that remain unresolved. For better or worse we are the inheritors of our passage into and through life. It is that passage, all be it overlaid and obscured by our ways of coping, which exerts the greatest influence on how we meet every event and crisis of life. For some that meeting uncovers a weakness which is only coped with by 'madness', by becoming sick. According to this model, all of us, the sane as well as the insane, are possessors of a psychopathology which differs not in kind, but in quality. It is possible to change this, provided treatment is directed to causes rather than effects, to the nature of our personalities rather than the symptoms of our distress.

In Chapter 4 David discovered something of the cause of his problems by remembering how his parents' conflict upset him. The car journey he so enjoyed became a nightmare of shame and guilt, a symbol for why he found it so hard to trust his own experience, and the cause of the warfare between his mind and body.

This model is one which appeals and repels. Its use of metaphor and symbol defies objective examination, for its truths cannot be scientifically verified. Nonetheless the painstaking application of theory to practice in case after case provides an alternative method of research.[12] At present this does not satisfy the critics of psychotherapy, but in time it may gain greater respect. It does, however, attract those disillusioned with trying to fit round man into the square holes of science, and for whom a respect for meaning and value makes implicit sense. Despite its apparent renunciation of much traditional religion, this model has much in common with religion. This is reflected in the many schisms which have adorned its development since Freud's original work.[13] In its application, that is in psychoanalysis and psychotherapy, its influence has been restricted. Understanding the psyche is a laborious and costly business available in practice to only a few. But the psychodynamic perspective has had considerable influence in a wide variety of spheres, from the upbringing of children and the care of the dying, to the management of organizations and selection into the armed forces. More specifically, it has had a major influence upon the development of the mental health professions, upon the counselling movement as a whole and pastoral counselling in particular.[14]

The behavioural model

This model is based upon the notion that every behaviour is the result of a chain of cause and effect. An individual's action is always the result of the influences, nice and nasty, which preceded it. If one effects changes or modifies those influences, then the individual's actions and behaviour will alter accordingly. Although the behaviourist draws upon the principles of experimental psychology and learning theory, he relies almost exclusively upon empirical evidence to justify his methods, and the model which he derives from them. He assumes 'madness', like everything else in human experience, is learnt, and that the phenomena of madness, the symptoms of illnesses, are logical responses to inadequate and unhelpful learning which can be altered and modified by relearning.

Children deprived of positive attention behave badly and so attract the negative attention of their parents. Over a period of time they learn that behaving badly is the way of not being overlooked. Relearning, according to behaviourist principles, would involve the withdrawal of attention for bad behaviour, and the reward of positive attention for good behaviour. The treatment techniques devolved from this model have been used with considerable effect upon particular problems and illnesses (e.g. mental handicap, compulsive, obsessive and phobic behaviour and sexual dysfunction). Emma in Chapter 2 was undergoing a behavioural treatment known as 'flooding' to help her grieve more fully than she had been able to do. The model itself has had a more general influence upon the way 'madness' is understood and managed. Psychiatric hospitals and units function broadly on behaviourist principles, by creating an atmosphere in which movement towards health is reinforced and rewarded, and illness, even by implication, is discouraged.

The advantages of this model are simplicity and pragmatism. It is relatively easily understood both by the treaters and treated, and its effects are quickly discernable. In the treatment of specific and identifiable behaviour problems it has been most successful, but is less so with problems of thinking and feeling, and with more complex psychiatric conditions. Like the psychodynamic model it attracts strong reactions. For some, its straightforwardness comes as a great relief after the mysteries of the other models. For others, its tendency to reduce man to the status of a machine carries neither charm nor conviction.[15]

The social model

> No man is an island entire of itself . . . Any man's death diminishes me, because I am involved in mankind; and therefore never send to know for whom the bell tolls; it tolls for thee.[16]

Much of the fear which surrounds 'madness' is like the fear of contagion. The essence, disease or spirit of the mad will, it is thought, catch and conquer others. A recently appointed psychiatric hospital chaplain, commenting on his experience, said: 'I have never been as exhausted as I am now. It is as if the misery, anger and fear of the mad has crept unseen into my own emotional blood stream.' Contagion is not an inappropriate metaphor, for the results of many social studies reveal that there is a relationship between the incidence of 'madness' and inadequate social, educational and environmental conditions. Mental breakdown and allied behavioural problems are high in communities where there is poor housing, low job expectation and satisfaction, inadequate social and educational facilities. There seems to be a striking correlation between mental illness and the number of significant relationships a person has; the more relationships the better we are. It is also clear that the concentration of treatment upon individual sufferers makes little difference to the numbers who are ill.

Revelations such as these prompted the development of a model of 'madness', more social than individual, and which could do greater justice to political, economic and social, as well as psychological and medical factors. At one extreme the adherents of this model proclaim that mental illness is a myth;[17] it is a figment of society's imagination, just as the devil was a myth for earlier generations. As a result the deviant, the strange and the disadvantaged can be coralled away in relative security and ignorance, while the rest of us get on with our lives safe from their contamination, and the distress they cause us. For others, the social model has given substance to the community psychiatric movement. The large and remote psychiatric hospitals are being emptied, patients are treated on a daily, more informal basis, sheltered accommodation and work are provided, and patients are re-integrated into their own communities and families. It is argued that, if society, its communities and groups, foster illness, then it must also be possible for society to foster health. The wounded, at least the mentally wounded, are the best healers, and their common desire for health can be harnessed by the appropriate management of their energies and their environment. More recently still the principles of the social model have been applied to one of our oldest and most powerful institutions, the family.[18]

The idea that individuals bear the sin, health and sickness of others within their group or family is not new. What is new, to our individually orientated society, is the rediscovery of the family's or group's involvement in illness. Family therapists look upon the illness of an individual family member as the symptom of that family's disease. For instance, a child's concern to 'save' his family from a real or imagined disaster can force upon him the crisis of becoming ill, in order that others will be well, or at least protected by his sickness from some greater evil. According to this model, Sarah's illness[19] was her attempt to rescue her family from something worse. So used had she become to this sense of responsibility, that she felt herself to be answerable for every disaster.

The social model is both benevolent and subversive. For some of its followers it is important to embrace and respect what is best in the other models. For others the change required is too great to be evolved, and only revolution will free the 'ill' and the 'healthy' from their unnatural and collusive alliance. The dilemma highlights the importance of the model. Its challenge to an excessive preoccupation with the individual is as important in pastoral care as it is in medicine. It asserts what seems all too obvious – 'no man is an island'. Each of us is both an individual and also part of a number of groups and systems within society. Attention needs to be given to the parts and to the whole, the individual and the group. The adherents of the social model struggle to devize methodologies which do justice to both.[20]

The medieval model

It is not suprising to find that attitudes to mental illness reflect the predominant contemporary views, be they religious, political or social. The notion that deviant behaviour is attributable to illness makes sense in a medically orientated culture, and that such behaviour is the work of the devil or some evil spirit fits a culture where religion dominates. In the case of Harry, in Chapter 3, two different cultures meet and conflict. The medical model of the hospital confronts the devil possession or religious model of 'madness' held by Harry, his family and his church. There is a long history to the religious model of 'madness', hence the term medieval. The evidence of the Old and New Testaments, the beliefs and practices of Christians through many centuries provide substance for the renewed interest in exorcism and spiritual healing. Whatever the alarms and uncertainties about this model, and there are many who have suffered terribly at its hands, there are others for whom it has brought healing and relief. It helps some people with some problems. Because it is the model which fits most uneasily into our contemporary culture, it illustrates well the problem inherent in all models;

namely the confusion between reality and how that reality is described and defined. As was emphasized earlier, 'madness' is for the most part mysterious and inexplicable; but that has encouraged, rather than impeded the forming of views, developing of hypotheses and the finding of ways to describe it. All the models of 'madness' have grown out of that attempt to describe and explain the mystery. Human nature, however, rarely rests content with such partial understanding. Descriptions, be they metaphorical symbolic or rational, come in time to replace that which they describe.[21] Schizophrenia, a term coined to describe a person exhibiting a particular set of symptoms, now has the status of an illness. Indeed people suffering from it are even called schizophrenics. And so, for Harry and his family, his experience of being possessed by the devil was more than a metaphorical description. It was the reality which evidence from another culture, using another language, could do little to dislodge.

A major contemporary manifestation of the medieval model is to be found lurking in a question often aroused by mental illness, especially when the behaviour of the ill person affects another person's rights, possessions or safety. Are the antisocially insane mad or bad, or something of both? This is a point at which different views of responsibility converge. Juries, judges and psychiatrists do not always see eye-to-eye. It was recently estimated that approximately one-third of prison inmates in the United Kingdom could be diagnosed as suffering from some psychiatric disorder, but few are likely to receive any treatment for it.[22] And there is no evidence to suggest that psychiatric patients are more prone to criminal behaviour than are the rest of the population. Attitudes towards the criminally insane reflect more emotion than reason, and show a plethora of assumptions and concerns. Some argue that there is always insufficient evidence to determine whether an individual is mad or bad, and therefore that all should be kept in the safe custody of prison or special hospital. Others claim the criminally insane to be the victims of severe social and psychological problems, and in need of intensive therapeutic treatment and care. Between these extremes, the growing speciality of forensic psychiatry strives to improve assessment and prognosis, and to clarify the best ways to treat different patients.

So much then for the models of 'madness'. Few who suffer from mental illness, or who care for and treat its sufferers, hold exclusively to any one model; that is the prerogative of those who keep their distance. In practice it is the medical model which predominates present-day psychiatry, despite recent attempts to dislodge it.[23] It provides the language and concepts which the other models use, if only to refute. It is to that model that we must turn for a fuller picture of mental illness today, and look at forms of mental illness within the two systems of classification generally used.

Classification 1

The first is a simple division into three broad categories, which are identifiable by the different reactions, feelings and behaviour experienced by the sufferers, and observed by those close to them. Many recognize a continuum of sanity to insanity, from normality through *neurosis* to *psychosis,* and use the term *personality disorder* for those conditions which cannot be placed in that continuum.

Neuroses

People suffering from neurotic illnesses are in touch with reality, relatively able to manage their lives, and yet have an abnormal or exaggerated preoccupation with themselves. Everyone is more or less neurotic about something – health, occupation, cleanliness, relationships, whatever. It is when such preoccupation begins to dominate a person's life that the notion of illness arises. For instance, it is relatively normal to have some anxiety about crossing a road, it is neurotic never to cross a road because one's anxiety is so great. Pam, Emma and Joan (in Chapter 2) were suffering from neuroses.[24] The majority of the mentally ill who claim the time and attention of the health services, either directly because of their nerves or indirectly because of worries associated with some physical complaint, come into this category. They are, for the most part, treated, not in hospital by psychiatrists, but in the community by the primary care services.[25] Churches and religious fellowships are often a major source of care and comfort to the neurotic.

Psychosis

A person suffering from a psychotic illness has lost touch with reality and, as a result, believes in and acts upon things which are completely false. Such people may claim to be someone else, or to be under the influence of someone or something for which there is no rational confirmation. For instance, a road is not crossed, not because of anxiety about traffic, but because the person's enemies have laid explosives beneath the tarmac. Edward and Sarah (in Chapter 2) were suffering from psychoses.[26] Such patients can be cared for within the community if there are adequate resources, but more often they are admitted to and treated in psychiatric hospitals or clinics.

Personality disorders

This term is used to apply broadly to those conditions which do not fit easily into either neurotic or psychotic categories: for instance, people whose behaviour not only deviates from the norm but also affects their own or other people's lives in some unacceptable way. Included in this category are those suffering from addiction to alcohol and drugs, those with sexual disorders and the criminally insane, who have committed offences and who are judged to have done so because of some major social or psychological problem. If neuroses are defined as transient disturbances of a part of the personality, personality disorders are the persistent disturbances of the whole personality. Ray (in Chapter 2) had a personality disorder.[27]

Classification 2

The second system is a more precise classification of illnesses, some of its categories spanning those in the first system, while others fit more naturally into one or other of them. Because of the problems of diagnosis, there is no internationally agreed classification of illnesses. The following provides a descriptive journey through the world of psychiatry, and a short-hand language to help the traveller understand the dialects. Some suggestions about the pastoral care appropriate to the sufferers, their relatives and helpers is included after a description of each illness.

Organic disorders

Organic disorders are those illnesses in which damage or deterioration to the brain can be identified by way of a brain scan or electroencephalogram (EEG). The minute electric currents coming from our brain cells can be recorded and their patterns mapped. This is done by placing small electrodes on a patient's head, and recording on a graph the brain impulses. When this is done, no external electric current is passed through the brain. Delirium is one such illness, and is typified by such symptoms as clouding of consciousness, lack of concentration, disorder of perception, illusions and visual hallucinations, mis-identification of people, and disconnected and incoherent speech. In its acute state, it is less difficult to diagnose than it is to identify the underlying causes. Inflammation of the central nervous system, sudden withdrawal of drugs or liver failure are some, among many, of the causes. The most common disorder is dementia. An ageing process in which the functions of the brain deteriorate, either because the blood supply to the brain is affected by diseased arteries (arteriosclerotic dementia), or the brain itself grows smaller and cells die, not to be replaced (senile dementia). Failing memory, especially for recent events, problems of comprehension and judgement, sudden and unaccustomed emotional irritability, loss of bladder and bowel function and carelessness in personal care are the symptoms of dementia. The illness may begin gradually, and respond to treatment for a time, or it may be rapidly progressive. There is no cure for it.

Harry (in Chapter 3) was suffering from senile dementia. His case illustrates the problems of this illness, for his own confusion, unhappiness and guilt are reflected in his relatives' misery, anger and resentment. A second 'childhood' is not always as welcome as the first. Heroic attempts to care for relatives at home have to be set against the possible dehumanizing effect of institutional care. The patient's life, though sometimes tolerable to them, is generally frightening and humiliating to their family and friends.[28]

Those involved in the care of a patient suffering from senile dementia have before them a formidable task. They have to help someone, whose intelligence is waning, to die. The temptation to avoid this frightening fact is often overwhelming and the patient's condition a convenient excuse. Managing such primitive and confusing emotions requires of us much self-understanding, and the willingness to share our own feelings with colleagues. For some there is a real purpose and satisfaction in caring for patients and their relatives. This is particularly true of those whose faith has matured through the buffets of life. For others there is horror and fear which may lead to denial or blame, and can certainly undermine relationships within and between families and institutions.

Pastors have a special contribution to make, for they represent something of the whole of the experience. They visit the sick and their relatives, meet with hospital staff and other helpers, bury the dead and minister to the bereaved. Furthermore, developing the attitude and skill of a counsellor will help the pastor to understand and contain the raw emotions, and help with their expression and resolution. By recognizing and eliciting people's hopes and fears, anger and love, despair and guilt, the pastor can give everyone the opportunity and security to confront the awefulness of death, and to find within themselves, and one another, the resources to bear despair and cherish hope.

Affective disorders

A change in mood is a common experience to most of us, some days we wake up happily and hopefully, on others we are anxious or bad-tempered. Affective disorders are so-called because they refer to those illnesses where a patient's mood has gone beyond what is usual, or is fixed in one or other extreme position. The patient's feelings preoccupy them to the extent that their pattern of life is seriously disrupted.

Depression

Depression is the most common illness in this group. It is often divided into those depressions traceable to some external cause or life event, which precipitated the sadness or despair (reactive depression) and those which come unheralded, and for which there seems to be no external cause (endogenous depression). The typical symptoms of depression include loss of appetite and sleep, inability to concentrate and remember, self-absorption and fears of all kinds. The feelings are of sadness, despair, guilt, self-blame, self-destruction and suicide. Joan, (in Chapter 2) and Leslie and Mary (in Chapter 4) all suffered from depression.

The major treatment for depression of both kinds is medical, namely the use of antidepressant drugs.[29] These are normally slow to work, but by alleviating the symptoms they help patients over the worst effects of the illness. There are a number of different antidepressants, and the matching of drug to patient can take time, often when the need for relief is greatest. Electro-convulsive therapy (ECT) is also used, principally because it can work more quickly than antidepressants. The side-effects of these treatments, particularly some memory loss, together with the natural apprehension about any treatment which does not immediately or may not ever help, contribute to a patient's anxiety and uncertainty. Psychotherapy and counselling (both individual and group), behaviour therapy and family therapy are all used, especially for those whose depression is thought to be reactive.

Suicide. Many who suffer from depression as well as other mental illnesses will consider and also attempt suicide. Of those with a psychotic depression about 15 per cent will successfully commit suicide, and one in ten of those who attempt to kill themselves will succeed. Factors associated with a high risk of suicide are recent widowhood or divorce, a family history of suicide, previous attempts at suicide, the onset or the end of an illness, agitation, insomnia and feelings of guilt and inadequacy. Men are more likely to do it than women, and those over forty more likely than those under forty. There is also evidence of the marked effect attempted suicide can have not only upon the individual themselves, but also upon all those involved with them, family friends and helpers. 'The relationship between the individual and society is renegotiated both positively and negatively, as if the suicidal attempt awakens both to the need for this renegotiation, which has gone unnoticed hitherto.'[30] Strongly held religious beliefs can deter individuals from attempting suicide, as in the case of Mary (in Chapter 4), but for others both the thought and the action can add to their guilt feelings and make it all the more difficult for them to approach their pastors.

The pastor's role with the depressed is a complex one. Being with a depressed person and listening to their misery and self-loathing is not easy. The weight of it can feel too heavy, and the pastor may unknowingly reinforce the patient's sense of worthlessness. The fact that depression does go, or at least lifts from time to time, is impossible to believe when it is at its worst. So the pastor who offers regular and continuing support, who allows and attends to the expression of what is most frightening, will help the most. To do this effectively pastors must take their own needs seriously. They must set limits upon the time they offer so that, while offering it, they give the whole of their attention. Furthermore they should consult colleagues who can help them assess and understand their work. The pastor who counselled Emma (in Chapter 2) provides a vivid example of how contagious depression can be. He caught Emma's sense of failure, and needed help to see it was hers and not his. Instead of carrying her misery away and burying it in his sense of failure, supervision helped him to understand how his feelings replicated hers. With that knowledge he could respond to her with even greater empathy.

In offering this kind of care the pastor provides a model for the patient's relatives and friends who need equal encouragement, both to do what they can, and to refrain from trying to do what they cannot. They, too, will feel angry and resentful, guilty and hopeless, and will fluctuate between over-involvement and guilty detachment. The pastor's early involvement and care at the most critical (often psychotic) stages of depression can provide a valuable foundation for later counselling. In particular pastors can help patients see where their religious beliefs may have reflected their problems or even exacerbated them, and how a healthier belief could contribute to their recovery.

Manic depression

One of the most alarming and confusing of affective disorders is manic depression. The patient suffering from this illness has dramatic mood swings, at times experiencing depressed periods, like those mentioned above, and at others a sudden euphoria, accompanied by a heightened sense of strength and ability. The manic periods are often the most noticeable, individuals can go without sleep for long periods, involve themselves in new and exciting activities, spend vast sums of money they do not possess, and start impossible projects which have no end. Difficult as depression is for both sufferers and their families, mania has more disturbing features. In religious people, it often takes the form of excessive evangelical zeal, involving grandiose plans to convert all those who come within range of the patient. The principal medical treatment is with lithium carbonate, which helps reduce the severity of the moods and the violence of the emotional swings. To achieve this requires some vigilance on the part of the doctor involved, to check the patient's lithium level, and to maintain the right dosage of medication. In the critical stages of the illness patients can be most unco-operative, because they feel very well. There is also a tendency for them to stop treatment once they have recovered from their depressive swing, so precipitating another cycle of illness.

The pastor's most valuable contribution to the care of the manic depressive is as an attentive observer of the patient's mood swings. By recognizing these, pastors can sense the onset of a manic phase, and distinguish it from normal involvement and interest in some activity. They can also take seriously the periods of depression, when the patient's withdrawal from company is easily ignored. The pastor's effective counsel and support can help the patient unlock the problems which aggravate the illness and precipitate the cycle of depression and mania.

Anxiety states

Few, if any of us, are strangers to anxiety. We worry about our health, our aging, our children, our parents, etc. and, recalling our Lord's injunction 'not to be anxious', we even worry about worrying. So it is not surprising that for some people anxiety reaches debilitating proportions. Those suffering from anxiety states speak of strange and sometimes violent bodily sensations. They are convinced of a heart attack, or some impairment to their breathing. They assume they are about to die, and despite thorough medical examinations, which reveal nothing, they still believe they are physically ill.

Obsessions and compulsions are the common features of the illness. In the case of the former, patients feel that their anxieties will only be managed if all of their time, attention and energy is given over to them. While in the latter, patients are compelled to act in certain ways in order to gain relief. For instance, they must continually wash their hands in order to avoid infection.

The most widely known of the illnesses are those termed phobias: agoraphobia is the fear of going out into open or busy places; claustrophobia is the fear of confined spaces. Many other phobias are associated with particular objects or sensations. As the sufferers will say, it is impossible to imagine the extent of their fear about things which do not disturb friends and relatives. They become frustrated and angry with themselves, so intensifying their anxiety and filling their lives with preoccupations, rituals and checking. The more they behave in this way the more they need to, in order to keep their anxieties under some control. Mary (in chapter 4) records her sense of panic and fear in this way.

Treatment for these conditions involves the use of medication to alleviate the more acute aspects of anxiety, and then either behaviour therapy or psychotherapy. Behaviour therapy has been particularly successful where the illness is focussed on a single problem. More difficult are those cases where the anxieties are less specific, and where there are associated illnesses like depression.

The pastor's role with these patients, their relatives and friends is primarily supportive: first by understanding how totally overwhelming the illness can be to patients, and how out of proportion it seems to others; and then by communicating that understanding to all those involved, in order that proper treatment can be sought and then accepted. Again Mary exemplifies the difficulties, both for patients and their relatives, in judging how serious things have to be before help is sought. Behaviour therapy involves frightening and sometimes distasteful procedures which patients can undertake only with encouragement and support. For instance treatments used for those with sexual problems often require patients to do things which are strange if not immoral to them. The pastor can often help both patient and therapist find an effective and ethically acceptable treatment. A young Jew who had a phobia about semen, and whose treatment required his masturbating, was greatly helped by his rabbi's involvement in planning his therapy.

Schizophrenia

Schizophrenia, literally 'the splitting of the mind' is one of the most emotive words in the vocabulary of psychiatry. Often used inappropriately and inexactly, it has come to stand for the popular stereotype of 'madness' – hearing voices, delusions, extraordinary and occasionally violent behaviour, irrational fears. These are the symptoms which characteristically separate the insane from the sane. And yet schizophrenia is not so much one illness, but rather the name given to a particular set or syndrome of symptoms. 'In our present state of knowledge our criterion for a diagnosis of schizophrenia can only be the presence of the typical clinical features of schizophrenia.'[31]

However, a number of international studies demonstrate how difficult it is for psychiatrists in different countries, as well as within the same hospital, to reach agreement on the diagnosis of these typical clinical features. Hence there is the growing belief that the term 'schizophrenia' is too vague, and that it embraces a number of different though not easily distinguished conditions. Edward (in Chapter 2) is a case in point. He exhibited some of the symptoms but not others. The common features of this illness or illnesses include the following: patients experience the control of their thoughts, emotions and actions by some alien body or person (for instance, thoughts are inserted, withdrawn or broadcast to others against their will). In a similar way they may hear voices (auditory hallucinations) talking about them in the third person, or have delusions about themselves being the object of other people's vengeance or admiration. Schneider[32] grouped these features together as the so-called 'first rank' symptoms of schizophrenia. He argued that their presence warranted its diagnosis, provided that tests eliminated the possibility of an organic brain disease or drug-induced psychoses.[33] Others, however, have been more cautious, pointing to the presence of these symptoms in other conditions.[34] In our pluralist society care should be taken to clarify the patient's world-view and cultural norms. Ideas which may appear delusional or experiences which sound hallucinatory need to be tested against the common currency of the patient's family and peers.

The illness often appears quite suddenly and traumatically in adolescents and young adults. Its distressing nature, together with the problems of diagnosis, has fuelled the fires of speculation about its cause and possible cure. It has been at the centre of many of the conflicts between those who hold different models of madness. Arguments have been assembled for genetic, organic, biochemical, social and psychological causes. Clare summarizes the results of this search for a cause: 'Not a lot of gold dust to show for over a century of painstaking observation, sifting and sieving of the mud of human experience.'[35]

Nevertheless, in the last twenty years, there have been remarkable changes in the care of those suffering from schizophrenia. Developments in the use of antipsychotic drugs have released many from permanent hospitalization, to lead more active lives within the community. Psychotherapy, and more recently family therapy, has helped reduce some of the pressures upon patients and their relatives. Therapeutic communities, halfway houses and sheltered workshops have given sanctuary and rehabilitation to many who were losing all sense of self respect and autonomy. In particular, the National Schizophrenia Fellowship[36] has been an effective vehicle for the pooling and disseminating of knowledge and understanding about the illness.

The patients' problems of commitment and basic trust, represented in their sense of isolation from reality and real people, affect their capacity for faith. They require sensitivity and consistency in care if that faith is to grow at all. This is an enormous challenge to pastors. Will they persevere with their commitment if they get so little in return? Will they stay to help trust develop, or turn away and so reinforce the patients' sense of despair?

The pastor's role with this, the most confusing and demanding of illnesses, is more than ever to be present, if possible in the crisis of the psychotic breakdown, when no one really knows what is happening, and then through the often long and distressing period of treatment. Pastors can demonstrate their willingness to try and understand. They can refuse to compound the patient's sense of isolation by their regular visits, their readiness just to sit and wait out the worst. They can offer the patient's relatives the same attention, and readiness to hear their confusion and fear, anger and humiliation. With others involved in treatment and care they can begin to see some picture of the significance of the illness: the form it takes, the kind of delusions or hallucinations and their effect upon the patient and relatives. Many have pointed to the blinding insight which suddenly erupts from a patient's bizarre behaviour or confusing monologue. One young patient's psychotic episode coincided with the news that his mother was dying of cancer. During that time he felt himself to be Jesus, who he believed could make his mother better. Pastors are best advised to keep to themselves insights gained in this period, and not to attempt to share them directly with patients. In time they may well help pastor and pastored make more sense of what the illness was about.

Hysteria

When we say that someone is behaving hysterically we usually mean that their feelings have got the better of them in some dramatic and uncontrollable way, for instance, that they cannot stop crying or screaming. Hysteria, the illness, though in practice very different from an hysterical outburst, has this one thing in common, namely the sense of an experience or trauma being unmanageable and out of control. Patients suffering from hysteria respond by completely disassociating themselves from the trauma. They unconsciously protect themselves from the anxiety or stress that they cannot bear. Amnesia and fits similar to epilepsy, but where no brain damage is identifiable, and paralysis of limbs, where no physical cause is manifest, are examples of this totally unconscious defence. Careful diagnosis is of the utmost importance in order to rule out some other physical or mental illness, but once the hysterical disorder is confirmed, then the utmost consistency in treatment is essential. This requires a concerted effort in two directions, first to ignore and so play down the hysterical symptoms, and secondly to actively encourage the patient to live as normal a life as possible.

The pastor's role, like that of others involved in care, is to help patients assume more and more responsibility for themselves. But it needs to be understood that this will take time and courage, and that gains will often be followed by relapses. Occasionally there will be exciting and significant changes. More often pastors will be drawn into a frustrating alliance with a patient, and find themselves giving more and more of their time and attention with less and less effect. The setting of firm limits, the careful ignoring of symptoms, and encouragement and praise for any sign of independence in the patient are the attitudes most helpful for the pastor to adopt. It is important to work closely with others who are involved, in order to maintain a consistency of approach. Those suffering from hysteria deceive not only themselves but those who go to their aid.

Psychosomatic disorders

Although we still know very little about the relationship between our minds and bodies, there is growing evidence of important connections. The study of some physical diseases has revealed significant emotional stress in sufferers; for instance, illnesses involving respiratory, gastric, cardiovascular, menstrual and reproductive organs, as well as cancer, leukemia, skin diseases, arthritis and migraine, have all been examined for possible psychomatic components. The problem which the division of medicine into specialities imposes is that physicians and surgeons are better at spotting physical and medical problems, and psychiatrists, emotional and mental ones. Once it has been established that the emotional stress accompanying a physical illness is more than one would expect, then it is important for patients to be helped to make sense of what their illness is telling them. Perhaps they need to succeed, to avoid or to overcome something. Their need has extended them too much and their body has called for a halt.

Pastors have a significant part to play, because they are

likely to be aware of the stresses affecting a patient's life. As they are not involved in the physical treatments they can listen for the significant things which emerge in casual conversation. Although patients may say they want to be overhauled and put back on the road with as few questions asked as possible, at another level the enforced respite of hospitalization gives them time to think about themselves. Our emotional drives are not easily modified, nor is it simple to make the connection between physical and mental stress. For some, back pains are easier to bear than are their weighty feelings. These people require sensitive support if they are to confront what they are doing to themselves. Pastors are best advised to listen, and to let patients explore themselves at their own pace, and to make their connections as and when they can.

Personality disorders

Psychopathy

This term is generally applied to those patients whose behaviour is abnormally aggressive, seriously irresponsible and antisocial, and for whom the possibility of another diagnosis (e.g. schizophrenia) has been excluded. Society is uncertain about the appropriate response to patients who exhibit this behaviour, should they be treated or imprisoned? A statement from the Butler Report, defining the ill as only those who can be effectively treated, illustrates how lawyers and psychiatrists are muddled and confused about these patients: 'such persons shall not be committed to hospital unless the court is satisfied that there is a relevant mental or organic illness or relevant psychological defect and that therapeutic benefit will result from hospital admission.'[37]

Treatments have included long-term support and counselling, to help patients gain some insight into their difficulties, and also to help them to anticipate problems and conflicts in the future. However, one of the major characteristics of these patients is their inability to anticipate the consequences of their actions, or to feel guilt for what they have done. Past and future are often severed from the present. Treatment in a therapeutic community, as at the Henderson Hospital and

Grendon Underwood Prison, have also been used with some success.[38] It is very difficult to determine in advance which treatment will help which patient, hence the dissatisfaction with such a vague term as 'psychopath'. Although the extremes of antisocial behaviour generally diminish with age, those with such tendencies may continue to wreak havoc with their families and marriages. Ray (in Chapter 2) shows some of the features and reveals some of the problems of this kind of personality disorder.

To say that pastoral care is both very difficult and very important is an understatement. Just as the individuals are isolated from the dreadful and traumatic events in which they have been involved, so too they can be isolated from other human beings[39] (see Ray's feelings about his wife and family). Their behaviour produces fear, distrust and distaste in those who would offer help, and the pastor cannot be immune from such feelings. No doubt they represent all too accurately the feelings which the patients have about themselves, and which they have buried as deeply as they can. It is not difficult to imagine the degree of pain involved in patients' attempts to uncover such feelings. They can only start to do this if they have experienced, from those close to them, a degree of acceptance and forgiveness to match their own pain and self-rejection. They cannot do other than test that acceptance to the limit. Can the pastor love what is most unlovable about them? Their families and friends will make complementary demands upon the pastor as well. Their involvement with these patients is often complex and confusing. To keep their 'whiteness' intact, families have a habit of perpetuating the 'blackness' of their black sheep. The pastors do well not to join in apportioning blame or jumping to conclusions. It is better that they offer their presence as symbolic of a search for forgiveness in the midst of anger and rejection. Effective pastoring in such a highly charged situation is never easy. Pastors will feel pulled and pushed, misunderstood, hopeless and frightened, and will be sorely tempted to find more satisfying work. And yet there is much which can be done, if firm limits are established between pastor and pastored, and close collaboration is maintained with other helpers. Thus the pastor's non-aligned and powerless role can provide the basis for a relationship to which patients can always return with the expectations of an understanding and honest acceptance.

Addictions

Research into the habit of drug-taking, including alcohol, and exploration of the similar 'addictive' dependencies of eating and gambling, and, conceivably, dependence on hospitals and religions, has led to the recognition that all addictions have one thing in common. 'The notion of dependence on a drug, object, role, activity or any other stimulus-source requires the crucial feature of a negative effect experienced in its absence . . . which may range from mild discomfort to extreme distress.'[40]

In this sense dependence is best understood as a continuum, stretching from something that many people experience, like the need for a cigarette or drink, to a state where the whole of one's life is orientated toward the source of the addiction and nothing else matters. This dependency may be physical or psychological or both. In practice it is rare for either the cause or the treatment of an addiction to be simple. Many factors, physical, mental, psychological and social, have to be examined in order to prevent a chain reaction in which the addiction changes but the dependency continues.

Treatment is generally divided into three phases:

1. The acute drug overdose requires immediate hospitalization and detoxification.
2. The suspected addict needs to be carefully assessed, and this is best done in an area drug-dependence clinic which will also provide advice and help with the withdrawal.
3. Long-term rehabilitation is the most difficult phase to complete successfully. Different hospitals and clinics have approached this in a variety of ways, and the evidence is inconclusive and not encouraging.

Different treatment regimes have tried total abstinence, maintenance dosages, intensive therapeutic community treatment of both paternalistic and democratic kinds, and long-term counselling at a clinic. All have proved successful in a small proportion of cases. The major factor to emerge is that short-term treatment in hospital or prison based upon total abstinence nearly always leads to relapse, whereas longer-term outpatient treatment is more often associated with eventual abstinence. The growth of multi-drug taking evident in the 1970s, and associated with the changing availability of drugs, has contributed most to the notion that it is dependency, rather than any particular addiction, which is at the heart of the problem.

Alcoholism. The major dependency illness in this country is alcoholism, but a question remains as to whether is is an illness at all. Certainly the disease model has helped bring the excessive drinker into relationship with those who offer help and understanding, rather than judgement. And at the same time it has helped the people most affected by the patient's drunken behaviour, family and friends, to see the patient as a person in need of care rather than condemnation. On the other hand there are many other kinds of behaviour, not regarded as illnesses, which can lead to physical illness and even death (driving dangerously for instance). And drinkers once at home in the 'sick role' can all too easily absolve themselves for all responsibility for their illness and for getting better. More often, however, the difficulty is to get heavy drinkers to admit they have a problem, and that they may be 'alcoholics'. Proper assessment at a clinic is required to determine whether or not they are physically addicted and the extent of any physical damage, to their kidneys for instance. Even the production of such evidence and the knowledge that more drinking can only make things worse will not necessarily convince an individual of his alcoholism.

Sufferers need a lot of understanding and encouragement if they are to seek and then continue with treatment. Most of all they will need the patient and consistent forbearance of helpers and friends, who recognize that their condition often has to get worse before it can get better. It is particularly difficult for families to watch one of their number dying of drink and destroying the family in the process, and to know there is little they can do until the patient turns for help. Alcoholics Anonymous and Alanon groups (for relatives)[41] provide important resources of support at all stages.

Total abstinence is still the preferred treatment for the majority of alcoholics, particularly when it is supported by long-term counselling, group therapy and membership of Alcoholics Anonymous. It is through such counselling that the nature of the dependency can be uncovered and its destructive power confronted. Behaviour therapy has also been used successfully to help the recovered alcoholic to build a new pattern of life, to avoid temptation and to handle stress is more constructive ways. More recently there has been a development, supported by research, particularly in the United States of America, of controlled or social drinking.[42] It is estimated that between 5 per cent and 15 per cent of all alcoholics can be helped to return to controlled drinking. Though this is still regarded as heresy in many quarters, there are a growing number of centres and clinics which offer this treatment to selected patients.

If psychopathy produces in helpers an active sense of revulsion, then addiction evokes a more passive but equivalent sense of disgust and despair. To die a drug addict or alcoholic is to die a very lonely death at the end of a long series of rejections and humiliations. To be a pastor to the addicted requires the shepherd's qualities of searching for and staying with the lost. Patience, firmness, consistency and, above all, long-sufferingness are the qualities most required. Following alcoholics on the downward path, letting them go and standing by their families as they let them go, waiting for them to make the first move towards recovery – all of this is a thankless task, and yet one that both patient and relatives need more than any other. The dangers for the carers are numerous. They will be deceived and drawn into inconsistency, and enlisted as allies to get just one more drink or one more shot. They will be flattered into believing that they alone really understand. By becoming the focus of the dependency they will gradually find that their charity has been exploited, even blackmailed out of them, to their own and their patient's loss.

Sexual disorders

Attitudes to sexual deviations and abnormalities have altered in the same way as attitudes towards addictions, and with the same residue of ambivalence and ambiguity. Sex, for all the publicity and exploitation which surrounds it, is very personal and intimate. Many people have enormous difficulty in admitting to themselves, let alone explaining to others, their sexual needs, fears and longings. And yet those needs do not disappear by being ignored in oneself, or envied or judged in others. The work of social scientists, such as Kinsey,[43] revealed the scale of sexual inadequacy and uncertainty, and the misery which that causes. Although this has led to improved and improving education, many are still stranded somewhere between their inherited attitudes, prejudices and fears, and contemporary pressure to conform to sexual permissiveness and athleticism. It is hardly surprising that confusion and uncertainty about sex leads, in turn, to a freezing of attitudes and emotions, as exemplified by David (in chapter 4). Often in the course of counselling he struggled to reconcile his homosexuality with his Christian beliefs.[44] Sexual dysfunction clinics which are attached to some psychiatric hospitals, sexual and marriage guidance counsellors, family planning associations and some general practitioners have helped to provide both sense and direction to the bewildered and lost.[45] Their work is based broadly upon the principle that, with help, individuals and couples can discover and understand their needs. They can find what is both satisfying and morally right for them, and can be released from the burden of comparing themselves with others. Bebbington summarizes recent developments in this way:

> The liberalization of values over the last twenty-five years has led to lifting of legal and cultural sanctions which define deviation, and has induced people to question the ethic by which a person with deviation so defined was persuaded towards treatment. As a result of relaxation of pressures without and within, many more such people are happy (sometimes flamboyantly so) to live with their deviation.[46]

Thus taboos, fears, resentments and rejections can be addressed, understood and even overcome; ordinary marriages and relationships given the chance to grow and flourish and a whole host of allied problems eased.

Sexual problems are often the most intimate and personal, and especially inhibiting and embarrassing to those with strong religious and moral convictions. Pastors will often meet with those who seem to be in difficulty, and yet who cannot express their need. For such people the pastor may be the one person whom they will trust to help them. The qualities of empathy and respect will help pastors provide the counselling people need, as the first step towards expert help. Pastors can also find out about, and build up their trust in, the treatment facilities available locally, in order that they refer appropriately and provide effective support to those who are treated. People will seek the help of those pastors whose confidence shows that they understand and accept their own sexuality.

Mental illness in children and adolescents

Psychiatric and child-guidance services provide for children who suffer emotionally, whose individual development is distorted, or whose behaviour causes concern to their families, schools or other caring adults. In most cases the behaviour or disorder is seen to be markedly different from the norm for that age of child, before such steps are taken. Although the disease model is least easily sustained with regard to children, nevertheless their problems are generally divided into the following categories.

Psychoses specific to childhood, e.g. autism

Autistic children have abnormalities of speech and response, poor concentration and no imaginative play. They are also aloof from and indifferent to other people, are rigidly attached to certain objects and are very resistant to change. Although there are similarities to the symptoms of schizophrenia, autistic children grow up into autistic adults. The majority require sheltered, if not institutional care, and it is estimated that one-in-six can be helped to manage ordinary school and work.

Psychoses similar to those of adults, e.g. schizophrenia

(See above)

Emotional disorders

In children these include anxiety, misery and unhappiness,

sensitivity and shyness, and extreme relationship problems, usually with siblings. Such disorders often announce their presence by way of phobic behaviour, obsessive or compulsive ritualization, for example, bed-wetting, school phobia and unnecessary repetition of simple acts. There is little evidence to suggest that these conditions in children develop into adult illnesses. As Graham[47] points out, depression in children is 'best viewed as a reaction to environmental circumstances rather than an illness'. Often a child's distress is the sign of unidentified problems elsewhere in the family or social group. Sarah (in Chapter 2) believed herself to be responsible for her family's problems.

Conduct disorders

The help of psychiatric services is also sought for those children whose behaviour affects others. 'Children, so designated, persistently and excessively lie, steal, disobey, truant, fight, set fires or display unacceptably aggressive behaviour.'[48] For such conditions to be designated as illness there must be evidence of the child's own suffering. For instance, not all delinquents can be said to have a psychiatric disorder. A part of normal adolescence is the struggle for independence, including the separating off of one's self from parents and authorities in order to find one's own authority. This leads to the kind of testing which adults have difficulty tolerating.

Other classifications

These are related to specific developmental delays, in reading or speech for instance, or are symptomatic, as are fits, disorders of speech and eating, and bed-wetting.

Anorexia nervosa

'The relentless pursuit of thinness is a desperate struggle for a self-respecting identity.'[49] Hill summarizes the significance of this pursuit for thinness in the following way:

> As opposed to a conforming manner during childhood, when remarkable compliance and anxiety to please were prominent, individuation during adolescence, and the

> necessity to develop autonomy causes serious psychic conflict, to which the pursuit of thinness [refusing to grow up] provides a solution.[50]

The course of the illness, which is very rare in boys, begins with a girl's apparently quite natural preoccupation with her weight. But this takes on a disproportionate importance as her real size and her self-image have less and less in common. She will refuse to eat properly and hide or throw away food. At times, when near to starvation, her control will break down and be replaced by massive gorging and vomiting, followed by a subsequent guilt at her offence to herself (bulimia nervosa). This illness does persist into, and can begin in, adult life.

The treatment and care of children and adolescents in all the above categories include those models already introduced in the discussion of adult illnesses. As already mentioned, the illness model is least satisfactory with the young. It is the practice of most adolescent and children's units and guidance clinics to provide a service which combines medical, social and psychological treatments. It is seen as important to elicit the knowledge and help of all who are near to or involved with the patient, at home, school and in the community. Family therapy, either on its own or in conjunction with other treatments, has been the most obvious example of this trend to identify help and care as well as illness and disorder within the child's whole environment. Often this provokes immense anxiety, concern and guilt, in the child's parents and teachers who feel they must be to blame for what has gone wrong. If, however, it is pointed out that the family have resources of their own to help and to heal, and as much if not more expertise than the professionals can muster, then a family's anxiety is turned on its head, and considerable therapeutic resources are harnessed.

Often the pastor, like a teacher or some other interested adult, is the first to see the signs of distress in a child, or in parents who are worried. At first it is difficult to separate the ordinary and natural distresses of growing up from something more critical. As Hill pointed out, delinquency is a normal part of adolescence, so too are many other peculiarities of behaviour which worry children themselves and their parents.

The pastor's ability to listen sensitively is never more important than with the young and those responsible for them. Often children's illnesses are a reflection of their anxiety about what is happening or not happening within their family. A school refuser, for instance, may have somehow identified and so absorbed the mother's fear of being left at home alone. So, too, adults fear that they are responsible for their children's problems, and feel obliged either to deny their guilt by blaming someone else or to own it all and be consumed by self-recrimination. For both the extra-parental figure, much like the grandparent of old, can be the bearer of enormous relief or terrifying judgement. Pastors need to be particularly sensitive to the latter, for even their mildest advice or questioning can be received as the fiercest condemnation. On the other hand their listening, acceptance and understanding of people's worst and most frightening feelings, their respect for the real authority of the family and their patient expectation of finding a way forward, will be very therapeutic.

The first visit of a child or family to a clinic or out-patient department, to say nothing of a child's coming into hospital, is frightening and humiliating. It will be a great comfort to families to know that they are supported by their pastor in taking this difficult step, that their feelings are acknowledged, and that the awfulness is not ignored; with such a foundation, tragedy can be turned to triumph. So often 'illness' of this kind within a family can represent the greatest chance they have to change, and to put right what has somehow gone wrong. Paradoxically the child's problem is the signal which alerts the whole system to its need for help, and provides the opportunity whereby that need can begin to be properly met.

Notes

1. John 10.20.
2. Sir A. Lewis, 'Medicine and the Affections of the Mind' *(British Journal of Medicine,* 1963), pp. 1549ff.
3. T. S. Szasz, 'The Myth of Mental Illness' *(American Psychologist,* 1960), p. 113ff; see also D. Ingleby, *Critical Psychiatry,* Penguin, 1981.
4. See Chapter 2, pp. 8–15; also E. Goffman, *Stigma*, Penguin, 1968.

5. The Royal College of Psychiatrists, Submission to the Central Manpower Committee about the distribution of medical staff within the National Health Service, 1974.
6. See also A. W. Clare, *Psychiatry in Dissent,* Tavistock, 1976.
7. F. Basagalia, 'Crisis Intervention, Treatment and Rehabilitation', in *Alternatives to Mental Hospitals* (Report of the European Workshop, MIND, London, 1980), part 2, pp. 12–14.
8. *Care in the Community: a Consultative Document on Moving Resources for Care in England.* Department of Health and Social Security, July 1981; *Mental Health and the Community* (Report of the Richmond Fellowship Enquiry), Richmond Fellowship Press, 1983; *Common Concern,* MIND, October 1983.
9. Clare, op. cit., p. 213.
10. B. Inglis, *The Diseases of Civilisation* (Hodder and Stoughton, 1981), p. 106ff.
11. S. Freud, *Complete Psychological Works,* Hogarth, 1953–74; see particularly vol. 12 – for formulations on the two principles of mental functioning, see pp. 218ff. See also J. Brown, *Freud and the Post-Freudians,* Penguin, 1961.
12. R. Rosser and W. Kingston, 'Research in Dynamic Psychotherapy', in P. Hill *et al.* (eds.), *The Essentials of Postgraduate Psychiatry* (Academic Press, 1979), pp. 725–9.
13. Brown, op. cit.
14. M. Jacobs, *Still Small Voice,* SPCK, 1982.
15. M. Argyle, *The Psychology of Interpersonal Behaviour*, Penguin, 1967.
16. John Donne, *Devotions,* XVII.
17. Szasz, op. cit.
18. A. C. R. Skynner, *One Flesh, Separate Persons,* Constable, 1976.
19. See Chapter 2, pp. 49ff.
20. Skynner, op. cit. and R. Laing, *The Politics of Experience and The Bird of Paradise,* Penguin, 1967.
21. R. Gill, 'A Sociological Response' *(Contact,* 45, 1974); on page 34 the author elaborates on the way in which metaphors come to take on the reality to which they point. 'A historical perspective for example . . . could show how Christian theology first built metaphor upon metaphor to help men organise their thinking about their experience of themselves and of the Holy: and then acquired such prestige and moral control that all the elaborations of its metaphors came to appear as identifications of what was actually there. Such a perspective, showing also how scientific metaphors in turn helped men organise their thinking, in turn acquired prestige, moral control and the status of real identifications, might help the minister to realise why the moral authority of theology has so often seemed to be threatened by that of science.'
22. J. Gunn, 'Criminal Behaviour and Mental Disorder' *(British Journal of Psychiatry,* 130), pp. 317ff.
23. A. Miles, *The Mentally Ill in Contemporary Society,* Oxford, 1981.
24. See Chapter 2, pp. 8–39.
25. Primary care is given by medical general practitioners, community

mental health nurses and social workers, National Health Service and voluntary day centres, and by befriending services often sponsored by local branches of MIND (the National Association for Mental Health).
26. See Chapter 2, pp. 48–63.
27. See Chapter 2, pp. 40–7.
28. Other organic diseases include epilepsy, Alzheimer's disease, Pick's disease, Huntington's chorea and Creutzfeldt-Jakob disease. Brain tumours can also cause symptoms of a similar nature, as can various infections of the central nervous system, e.g. encephalitis, abcesses, syphilis and parasites.
29. M. Lader, *The Mind Benders: the Use of Drugs in Psychiatry,* MIND, 1981.
30. J. H. Foskett, 'To Be or Not To Be', in E. Shepherd and J. P. Watson (eds.), *Personal Meanings* (Wiley, Chichester, 1982), p. 97.
31. R. E. Kendall, 'Schizophrenia: the Remedy for Diagnostic Confusion' (*British Journal of Hospital Medicine,* 8, 1972), pp. 383ff.
32. K. Schneider, 'Primary and Secondary Symptoms of Schizophrenia', in S. Hirsh and M. Shepherd (eds.), *Themes and Variations in European Psychiatry,* Wright, Bristol, 1957.
33. Amphetamines and LSD, when injected, can cause psychosis.
34. R. Murray, 'Schizophrenia', in Hill *et al.* (eds.), *Essentials of Postgraduate Psychiatry,* pp. 349ff.
35. *A. W. Clare, Psychiatry in Dissent* (Tavistock, 1976), p. 213.
36. The National Schizophrenia Fellowship is a national organization for all matters concerning the relief of sufferers from schizophrenia and of their families and dependants.
37. Hill *et al.* (eds.), op. cit., p. 542.
38. S. Whitely, 'The Psychopath and His Treatment' *(British Journal of Hospital Medicine,* 3, 1970), pp. 263ff.
39. See Chapter 2, p. 42.
40. M. A. H. Russell, 'What is Dependence?', in Edwards *et al.* (eds.), *Drugs and Drug Dependence,* Lexington, 1976.
41. Addresses and telephone numbers for these organizations can usually be found in local telephone directories.
42. R. Murray, 'Alcoholism', in Hill *et al* (eds.), op. cit., p. 340.
43. A. C. Kinsey *et al., Sexual Behaviour in the Human Male* and *Sexual Behaviour in the Human Female,* Saunders, Philadelphia, 1948 and 1953.
44. See Chapter 4, pp. 70–2.
45. Addresses and telephone numbers of Family Planning Clinics and Marriage Guidance Councils can usually be found in local telephone directories.
46. P. Bebbington, 'Sexual Disorders', in Hill *et al.* (eds.), op. cit., p. 247.
47. P. J. Graham, 'Depression in Pre-Pubertal Children' *(Developmental Medicine and Child Neurology,* 16), pp. 340ff.
48. Hill (ed.), op. cit., p. 117.
49. H. Bruch, *Eating Disorders,* Routledge and Kegan Paul, 1974.
50. Hill (ed.), op. cit., p. 135.

Further Reading

Melville, J., *First Aid in Mental Health,* Allen and Unwin 1980.
Miles, A., *The Mentally Ill in Contemporary Society.* Martin Robertson, Oxford, 1981.
Oates, W., *The Religious Care of the Psychiatric Patient.* Westminster, Philadelphia, 1978.
Skynner, R. and Cleese, J., *Families and How to Survive Them.* Methuen 1983.
Wilson, M., *Health is for People.* Darton Longman and Todd 1975.

EIGHT

Theological Meaning in Madness

> The more I deal with the experience of the mentally ill, the more I am convinced that in so far as we attain to any true understanding of them, so far shall we be able to see the meaning and end of human life, both individual and collective. And in so far as we attain to such understanding, we should be well on our way toward building the city of brotherhood and co-operation on the place where the jungle now stands and greed and ruthless competition rule.[1]

This book has been about 'madness'. It has drawn upon the experience of those who suffer mental illness, and those, particularly pastors, who attempt to care for and help those sufferers and their relatives and friends. It has not painted an optimistic picture, for 'madness' continues to overwhelm the vulnerable, and to defy the many and painstaking attempts to stem the tide of its effects. 'Madness', far from going away or being cured remains to taunt and bewilder us, and to consume more and more of our resources, our concern and our limited expertise. Small wonder that we see it as an enemy which, if it cannot be defeated, has at least to be held at bay. As pastors, carers and counsellors, we too are summoned forward to the front line to make our contribution to this battle: to see in 'madness' the work of the devil, an evil which we have unique resources to counter. Edward and Sarah (in Chapter 2) conveyed their belief in the evil which was taking them prisoners and their hope in, but fear for, those who came to their rescue. The other stories in Part One tell a similar tale, of the mysterious pointlessness of mental illness, the pain of which is so much less specific and yet so much more intolerable than physical pain. The chapter on psychiatry revealed a similar picture of the destructive nature of 'madness' to helpers and helped alike. Psychiatry has discovered comparatively little about either the causes of or the cures for mental illnesses. Much more needs to be done to make the best use of what has been learned, and there is a tremendous need for more generous and adequate resources to be given to this Cinderella of the Health Service. Suffering of this kind and proportion is an offence without place or purpose and those who suffer unite with those who care for them in a common shame, frustration and despair. It is these emotions, among many others, which give the greatest weight to the view that 'madness' is a suffering without value.

The Judaeo-Christian tradition, however, challenges any such view, and Jews and Christians persist in searching for meaning in suffering. History and experience has taught them that suffering cannot be defeated and that there is more to it than what is most obvious and most distressing. Each has given to suffering a central place in their theology: for Jews, the exile and enslavement; for Christians, the crucifixion of Christ. It is this search for meaning in suffering which theology affirms, and especially in relation to those sufferings which appear to have least meaning. Mary, in her fight with 'madness' had this to say,

> I had battled for seven or eight years to stop the illness conquering me, and I'd given up the battle only to find that the illness could not defeat me, that I could in fact beat the illness, but by peaceful means. Perhaps the fight was important too. Certainly I don't think I would have learnt so much if I hadn't gone right through the whole experience.[2]

St Mark, in his Gospel, records how the disciples were brought face to face with this unnatural and inhuman view of suffering. They had come, through their experience of Jesus to recognize his uniqueness, that he was more than one of the prophets and greater than John the Baptist. At Caesarea Philippi, Peter went on to declare, 'You are the Christ,' meaning that he saw Jesus as the Messiah, the one who was to bring in the Kingdom of God, envisaged as a time of peace without pain and conflict. Then Jesus ordered his disciples to tell no one of their knowledge.[3] His reasons for this remain mysterious, and yet commentators have pointed to what he then went on to reveal about himself. They suggest that he was anxious not to reinforce the popular and partial view of

God's kingdom or of his own role as Messiah, but instead to help them grasp a truth which they would find both offensive and unacceptable.

> He began to teach them that the Son of man [a much more ambiguous and mysterious title than Christ] must suffer many things, and be rejected by the elders and the chief priests and the scribes, and be killed, and after three days rise again.[4]

The disciples wanted a superhuman Christ, a Messiah unaffected and invulnerable, who went about doing good and healing all manner of disease. Nineham explains in his commentary,

> They did not *want* Jesus to suffer, and that was because it goes against the grain to be followers of a Messiah who suffers instead of producing spectacular victories by an effortless exercise of power, it brings no kudos and offends the pride of natural man.[5]

Here Christian theology points to a different view of suffering, 'The Son of Man *must* suffer' argues that it is somehow in the nature of things that he *must.* His suffering does have a meaning and a purpose, and it would be wrong, indeed Peter was wrong, to suggest that he should avoid it. The Gospel goes on to record how difficult it was for the disciples to accept this point of view, which was so different to the one they held, namely that suffering was bad and therefore meaningless. In saying to Peter, 'You are not on the side of God, but of men,'[6] Jesus put his finger upon the crucial difference between the natural, most obvious way of viewing suffering, and the way that he was to reveal its meaning by his own suffering and death. Of course, this was only a beginning, not only was he to repeat this unacceptable message on a number of occasions but they were to remain consistently deaf to it. Even when he fulfilled his words by his actions, when he came to suffer and die, they still did not understand. His passion was a mystery to them, even as it happened before their eyes. The pointlessness obliterated all other reactions to it, and left them trembling behind closed doors, unable to reorder their lives around the reality they could no longer deny. The suffering of 'madness' often provokes a similar sense of offence. 'During the Good Friday office I was just sitting there crying right the way through, thinking, "Well, everyone is tripping these things off their tongues, but what do you do when it's you?" '[7] Meaning is rarely, if ever, apparent in the experience of suffering itself. Of its nature, suffering pushes all else out of the way and demands to be taken seriously, to be borne for its own sake. Philosophizing, even theologizing, about suffering is possible only to those who are at one remove from it.

> Sermons made me angry, and a religious tape about the joy of suffering. I switched it off. What in God's name did they think they were talking about? If there was any joy there wouldn't be any suffering.[8]

St Mark records Jesus foreseeing this:

> If any man would come after me, let him deny himself and take up his cross and follow me. For whoever would save his life will lose it; and whoever loses his life for my sake and the gospel's will save it.[9]

Suffering which can not be defeated cannot be left out or ignored. As it was a *must* for the Son of Man, so it is a *must* in some way for each one of us. Our sufferings, like our mistakes, are part of us, somehow as much at the centre of our lives and our vocation as the Son of Man's passion and crucifixion were at the centre of his. Harry Williams, a sufferer from mental illness, describes his reaction to the four figures sculpture by Michelangelo on the tomb of Pope Julian in the Academia di Belle Arte in Florence,

> Those four figures are us, as we are being torn out of non-being into being by the hammer blows of our experience, and we are being created, not in spite of the blows, but because of them. Yet no more than the rough stone do we know what we are being hit into — what form or pattern of beauty is being revealed by the marks of the chisel. Yet a time may come when we are able to feel that somehow the experience of hammer and chisel was worth it, that experience has not after all reduced us to a mess of meaningless bits and pieces but has provided us with a

> value and richness we should otherwise have lacked, so that our suffering is now seen to be woven into our joy as an essential part of it.[10]

There is a recurring question among those who pastor, and particularly among those who have in some way embraced the insights and qualities referred to earlier in this book. What is the special contribution that the pastors bring to care and counselling, over and above what is offered by secular helpers? No doubt the question springs from the insecurity that pastors feel about their failure to be any better than, and often not as good as, others at alleviating suffering. Certainly the question implies an expectation of superiority, that a pastor's care really is, or should be better than anyone else's. The point, however, is not that pastors have more to offer or that they are better at helping, but rather that they have access to a revolutionary perspective on suffering. The fact that they have less to help with (social and health services can muster more resources, techniques, cures and treatments), can, paradoxically, free them to stand for that perspective and to have it reveal its good news to those oppressed by 'madness',

> This theme in the Gospel suggests something important about pastoral counselling. Its ultimate goal is not healing, but revelation. In fact, healing may not be involved at all. It is not unlike the relationship between Jesus and his disciples presented in Mark where the whole story about life and God is gradually being revealed. Healing is not a way around the sin and brokenness in life. It is, rather, a witness to the fact that the power of God is present in the midst of brokenness, whether that brokenness is experienced as anxiety, sickness or death. Jesus' disciples discovered that there was always more of the story to be unfolded.[11]

A number of contemporary theologians have begun to suggest some ways in which theology, and pastoral theology in particular, can help us to make more of this unique contribution. Jenkins, in an article entitled 'Theology and the National Health Service'[12] examines the false hopes and expectations built up around the 'idol' of a health service, which it was expected would contain and gradually mop up disease. Its failure to do so is only just beginning to show us how imprisoned we are by an idolatory of science (medical science in particular). Cautiously, like explorers on a new planet, we are preparing to consider alternatives to medicine, and to see in suffering itself something more than an evil to be defeated. Selby takes up the theme of idolatry in an unpublished article entitled 'The one and the many – the transcendent in pastoral care'. He points out that:

> Those who take upon themselves the care of persons are constantly confronted with situations to which pastoral care is no solution. No activity is more likely to expose the inadequacies of the idols of individualism than a profound concern for individuals. Pastoral care has the capacity to give access to the transcendent, it points those who give and those who receive it beyond the problems which can be tackled by the pastor [or any other helper] towards the whole range of issues that have to be faced in the quest for an inclusive and just, responsible and loving human fulfilment in the Kingdom of God.[13]

A number of recent articles in *Contact* by Elford, Pattison and Dyson,[14] while not minimizing the difficulties, have laid claim to pastoral theology's importance in helping confront the enormous issues facing society today.

> It is possible to begin critically relating pastoral theology on the one hand, to fundamental theology and on the other hand to social and political arrangements about us. It is possible to see how, without ceasing to learn from other disciplines, without retiring from the fray, it is quite possible on a Christian argumentation to come up with a direction of social policy which is radically untypical of current practice, but which cannot be ignored simply because it differs from the prevailing wisdom.[14]

The time is ripe for theology to make its contribution, not in competition to that of other contributors, but as one perspective among many which all seek the truth. Theology needs to be reordered and renovated in order that it can be heard and understood; for too long it has been monopolized by university departments of theology, and now it has to be set free for all to use. What better place is there to begin than where society's shoe pinches the most, with those whose suffering drives them to search for its meaning. The metaphor of revelation is a better vehicle for describing the goal of pastoral care and counselling than is the metaphor of healing. The latter is strongly associated with medicine's assumptions of treatment and cure, whereas revelation is more exclusive to theology, and conveys its central conviction that God is in all things waiting to be found. So it was that the disciples were told that in visiting the sick, the prisoners, the poor, and so on, they were visiting God.[15] The mystery of suffering, like the mystery of God, is not in the end to be defeated or captured, but followed and discovered. Sufferer and carer should not be so distracted by either the hurting or the healing to miss what is even more significant than either the wounds or the bandages. The stories in Chapter 2, although only incomplete fragments provide us with the kind of hints so common to the work of revelation.

Pam's doubts emerging in a question about her sanity, prompted her to look for solid ground on which to rebuild her trust, something or someone who would take her doubts seriously. Joan reluctantly confronted her despair with herself and, finding that she could not provoke her pastor to a similar act of rejection, began to see in her pastor's faith some hope that there could be more to her story than her present worthlessness. Emma, like so many, felt unforgivable. Her suffering challenges the shallowness of much that purports to be repentance and pardon. She knows, at first hand, how difficult it is to placate the unforgiving part of herself. Her story could lead her to plumb the depths of atonement and justification by faith rather than works. Ray, like the psalmist, is acquainted with grief and rejection; 'I have become a stranger to my brethren, an alien to my mother's sons.'[16] His suffering, like many of the redundant in our society, has a prophetic appeal to it. Though he may deserve the rejection of his family, he has a right to expect more of the Church. 'Look, brother, Jesus accepted people immediately, and taught his disciples to do that.' He wants a church for sinners and not saints, a faith that admits his anger and bitterness, his knowledge that he is not alone responsible for what has happened to him. The sufferings of Sarah and Edward are a poignant reminder of the depths of human experience illustrated in the book of Job and in the Psalms. 'Save me, O God! For the waters have come up to my neck. I sink in deep mire, where there is no foothold.'[17] Their suffering strikes at the very roots of faith, questioning whether or not there is a fundamental unity and consistency to creation. They face the awesome dualism, which either tears them apart from within, or irretrievably separates them from everyone else. Their illness has them test every possibility, unpick every explanation, devour every authority, particularly religious authorities like the Bible, for evidence to confirm their worst fears. They test to the limit St Paul's affirmation, 'For I am sure that neither death, nor life . . . nor anything else in all creation, will be able to separate us from the love of God in Christ Jesus our Lord.'[18] Harry's story is one of loss and of losing, and of how difficult it is to find meaning in the pain of such unwelcome but inevitable experiences. Yet meaning there was and is. Once the distress was contained and then better understood, Harry's suffering could become the opportunity of revelation, to family and friends, hospital and church. We left the Faith and Doubt group pondering on the realization that our mistakes, however uncomfortable and unavoidable, are in the end a part of us, and the part from which we often learn and gain the most. Put another way, it is our sins which convince us of our need for salvation, and which therefore provide the reason and the impetus for our search to begin.

Mary and Leslie and David's stories speak for themselves, of the journey inwards to the wilderness of the soul, of the fight 'to wrest some meaning out of the loneliness, the silence, the inner emptiness, the suffering, the poverty, the spiritual dryness and the knowledge that knows nothing'.[19] They illustrate both the costs and the rewards of their fight to wrest some meaning out of their suffering and, like Jacob at Penuel to gain blessing as well as injury for their efforts.

Harry Williams, writing of his own breakdown, describes how meaning gradually dawned upon him:

> Human suffering, the more of a dead end it feels like, the more it is an invitation to join in Christ's sufferings, and in Him to bring light and life and healing and liberty to

mankind. So the cruelly destructive nature of suffering can be seen, if only in a glass darkly, as charged with positive and creative possibilities. Of course it isn't calculable. It's a mystery, which means it's too real for precise definition . . . It came to me with overpowering force: 'I am now eating Christ's broken body and drinking his outpoured blood. The service of Holy Communion in church is only a rehearsal, like military manoeuvres. But this I am going through now, this is for real.'[20]

In his book *Love's Endeavour, Love's Expense,* Vanstone explores this vision of suffering still further into the very person and nature of God himself. He began his ministry in the belief that the Church's task was primarily pastoral, to care for the material, emotional and spiritual needs of people. When he came to a new parish, he discovered that other institutions now did these things quite satisfactorily, and there appeared to be nothing for the Church to do. His own distress revolved around the question, what then was the Church for, if it was not to care for others? His efforts to find or make an answer got him nowhere, until one day in one of those moments of revelation an answer of a kind was given to him. Two boys in the parish made a simple model out of the odds and ends he gave them. He watched their creation take shape out of this very indifferent material and their involvement develop. At times they were very active, at others they seemed to be waiting, allowing for the paint to dry and for them to see if the model looked all right. Creators and created were locked together in a mutual endeavour, and 'the two boys became vulnerable in and through that which, out of virtually nothing, they had brought into being'.[21] Vanstone lists the three things which he learnt from this experience. First, that creation involves both working and waiting to see what emerges from one's efforts. Secondly, that 'the creator gives to his workmanship a certain power over himself'. And thirdly, 'that in such activity, disproportion between creator and workmanship, or between creator and material are overcome by the gift of value'. The thing which was nothing in itself, was transformed by creation into something of value.

For the self giving [of the two boys] built into the model, I

> could find no simple word or name but love . . . It was love which had given importance to the sticks and stones, and to myself, a sense of responsibility for them. I, the observer, perceived the importance of the model, and my own responsibility for it, because I know it to be a work of love. I had actually seen the activity of love.

Vanstone conceives of God as the creator who gives himself in his work of love, working and waiting, celebrating triumph and retrieving tragedy. And that our response to him is as essential in this endeavour as his gift to us. There is mutuality and interdependence between creator and created. The Church exists as the observer to and carer of this incredible activity, responsible for bearing witness to this activity of love. Sitting with the depressed, visiting the chronically demented, restraining the mentally handicapped from self-injury, are the human sticks and stones, the unlikely raw material of love's activity. If we can look more closely, feel more deeply, the strains and stress, the giving of love in those who suffer and in those who care for them, 'there', Boisen believed, 'we shall be able to see the meaning and the end of human life'. It is not surprising that we turn away from such a God, whose friends are the poor, and the sick, the hungry and the destitute. And yet the evidence of suffering suggests that it is they who bear its vocation, whose pain cannot be ignored but has to be embraced and transformed. They are the spiritual explorers of our age, traversing desert and wilderness like the mystics and hermits of old. Unfortunately we offer them more pity than reverence. Salvation and health will slip through our hands unless we can learn from them that we have to be sick in order to be really well. Ironically it is economic pressures rather than human or theological ones which will convert us to this way of seeing things. Today's emphasis on community rather than institutional care for the mentally ill, will help bring them back amongst us. The gap between the so-called sick and healthy will be narrowed, and it will be much more difficult to tell the difference between us and them. Then perhaps it will be easier for them to take us by the hand, and lead us to where they have been – for them to show us the activity of love, the work of finding meaning in 'madness', which is as much our work as theirs, for the Kingdom's sake.

Notes

1. A. Boisen, *Religion in Crisis and Custom,* Harper, New York, 1945; see also *American Journal of Pastoral Psychology,* September 1968, p. 48.
2. See Chapter 4, p. 89.
3. Mark 8. 27–30.
4. Mark 8.31.
5. D. Nineham, *Saint Mark* (Penguin Books, 1963), p. 226.
6. Mark 8.33.
7. See Chapter 4, p. 91.
8. As above, p. 91.
9. Mark 8. 34–5.
10. H. A. Williams, *True Resurrection* (Mitchell Beazley London, 1972), p. 145.
11. J. Patton editorial *(The Journal of Pastoral Care,* June 1982), p. 74.
12. D. Jenkins, 'Theology and the National Health Service', Part II *(William Temple Society Bulletin,* no 7, 1978). Jenkins says that it was out of pastoral concern for the mentally ill that he tried to understand what was 'going on between the medical profession and society, and in the functioning of the National Health Service . . . It is a necessity of faith to come to grips with that which gets so many people into its grip and shapes their lives at critical moments of distress and unease. If one believes that Jesus Christ is, in some real and lasting sense, "Saviour and Lord", then it is necessary to be able to understand those processes in contemporary society which are looked to by members of society for "healing" (which is closely linked to "being saved"). Further, the institutions society has fashioned for the provision of health and healing have developed their own features and autonomous power-structures which "lord it" over those who become subject to them, dependent on them and look to them for "health and healing".'
13. P. Selby, 'The One and the Many – the Transcendent in Pastoral Care' (unpublished paper).
14. Articles in *Contact: the Interdisciplinary Journal of Pastoral Studies,* 1983: in vol. 78, A. O. Dyson, 'Pastoral Theology Towards a New Discipline'; in vol. 80, J. Elford, 'Pastoral Theology at Manchester University', and S. Pattison, 'Pastoral Studies: Dust Bin or Discipline?'
15. Matthew 25. 31–46.
16. Psalm 69.8.
17. Psalm 69. 1–2.
18. Romans 8. 38–9.
19. J. Moltmann, *Experiences of God* (SCM 1980), p. 61.
20. H. A. Williams, *Some Day I'll Find You* (Mitchell Beazley, 1982), pp. 177–8.
21. W. H. Vanstone, *Love's Endeavour, Love's Expense* (Darton Longman and Todd, 1977), pp. 32ff.

Further Reading

Campbell, A., *Rediscovering Pastoral Care.* Darton Longman and Todd 1981.
Fowler, J., *Stages of Faith.* Harper and Row, San Francisco, 1978.
Grainger, R., *Watching for Wings: Theology and Mental Illness in a Pastoral Setting.* Darton Longman and Todd 1979.
Selby, P., *Liberating God.* SPCK 1983.
Taylor, M., *Learning to Care.* SPCK 1983.
Vanstone, W. H., *The Stature of Waiting.* Darton Longman and Todd 1982.

Useful Addresses

The following list is of some of the organizations which are involved in the work covered by this book.

Counselling

British Association for Counselling, 37a Sheep Street, Rugby, Warwickshire CV21 3BX (tel. 0788 78328). For information about counselling and counselling training throughout the United Kingdom.

The National Marriage Guidance Council, Herbert Gray College, Little Church Street, Rugby, Warwickshire (tel. 0788 73241). For marriage counselling and training: branches nationwide.

Pastoral care and counselling

The Association for Pastoral Care and Counselling, 37a Sheep Street, Rugby, Warwickshire CV21 3BX (tel. 0788 78328). For information about pastoral care and counselling and training throughout the United Kingdom.

Clinical Theology Association, St Mary's House, Church Westcote, Oxford OX7 6SF (tel. 0993 830209). A pastoral care and counselling network and training scheme.

The Church of England. A number of dioceses have pastoral care and counselling schemes, which can be contacted through the appropriate diocesan office.

The Dympna Centre, 24 Blandford Street, London W1A 4HA (tel. 01 486 1592). A counselling centre for clergy and religious of all denominations.

The Raphael Centre, 100 Ashmill Street, London NW1 6RA (tel. 01 289 7002). A Jewish counselling centre.

The Richmond Fellowship, 8 Addison Road, London WI4 8DL (tel. 01 603 6373). For training in pastoral care and counselling. Some courses are based upon practical placements in half-way houses for the mentally ill.

The Salvation Army Counselling Service, 177 Whitechapel Road, London E1 (tel. 01 247 0669). A counselling service and training scheme.

The Westminster Pastoral Foundation, 23 Kensington Square, London W8 5HN (tel. 01 937 6956). A counselling service and training agency for counsellors. There are a number of affiliate centres nationwide.

Religion and medicine

The Churches' Council for Health and Healing, St Marylebone Parish Church, Marylebone Road, London NW1 5LT (tel. 01 883 1831).

The Church of England Hospital Chaplains' Council, Church House, Dean's Yard, London SW1P 3NZ (tel. 01 222 9011). For training.

The Hospital Chaplains' Fellowship (c/o address as above).

The Institute of Religion and Medicine, 55 St Giles', Oxford OX1 3LU. An organization to promote better understanding in the field of religion and medicine. Local groups nationwide.

Pastoral theology

The following universities have departments of practical or pastoral theology: Aberdeen, Birmingham, Cardiff, Edinburgh, Glasgow, Hull, London and Manchester.

Mental health

The National Health Service. All district services have a department of psychiatry or psychological medicine. Contacts are best made with the consultant psychiatrist or social worker, and for in-patient units with the sister or charge nurse. The hospital chaplain will also provide help with referrals.

MIND, (The National Association for Mental Health), 22 Harley Street, London W1 (tel. 01 637 0741). A voluntary organization providing information, casework, advice, befriending, accommodation, and a legal and welfare rights service, through a network of local groups nationwide.

Scottish Association for Mental Health, 11 St Colme Street, Edinburgh (tel. 031 225 4606).

Northern Ireland Association for Mental Health, Beacon House, University Street, Belfast (tel. 0232 28474).

Specialist groups

Age Concern, Bernard Sunley House, 60 Pitcairn Road, Mitcham, Surrey (tel. 01 640 5431). Advice and information about services for the elderly.

Al-Anon Family Groups, 61 Great Dover Street, London SE1 (tel. 01 403 0888). For support and advice for the families and relatives of compulsive drinkers.

Alcoholics Anonymous (AA), PO Box 514, 11, Redcliffe Gardens, London SW10 (tel. 01 352 9779). Self-help groups for alcoholics and heavy drinkers.

CRUSE, Cruse House, 126 Sheen Road, Richmond, Surrey (tel. 01 940 4818). Provides clubs and a counselling service for the bereaved.

Depressives Anonymous, 21 The Green, Chaddersley Corbett, Kidderminster, Worcestershire.

Depressives Associated, 19 Merley Ways, Wimbourne Minster, Dorset (tel. 020 125 3957).

Gamblers Anonymous, 17/23 Blantyre Street, Cheyne Walk, London SW10 (tel. 01 352 3060 or 368 0316).

Gingerbread, 35 Wellington Street, London WC2 (tel. 01 240 0953). A self-help organization for one-parent families.

Institute of Behaviour Therapy, 22 Queen Anne Street, London W1 (tel. 01 444 6030). Provides treatment for phobias, obsessions and stress management.

National Schizophrenia Fellowship, 78 Victoria Road, Surbiton, Surrey (tel. 01 390 3651). For advice and support for sufferers and relatives.

The Schizophrenia Association of Great Britain, Tyr Twr, Llanfair Hall, Caernarvon, Gwynedd, North Wales (tel. 0248 670 379).

Open Door Association, c/o 447 Pensby Road, Heswall, Merseyside (tel. 051 648 2022). A self-help organization for those suffering from phobias and anxiety states.

Samaritans, 17 Uxbridge Road, Slough, Berkshire (tel. Slough 32713). A listening and befriending service for the suicidal and those in distress. See local telephone directory for the nearest branch.

Patients' rights

Citizens' Advice Bureaux, 110 Drury Lane, London WC2 (tel. 01 836 9231). See local telephone directory for the nearest local office.

Citizens' Rights Office, 1 Macklin Street, London WC2 (tel. 01 405 4517). For practical help and advice on welfare rights.

National Council for Civil Liberties, 186, Kings Cross Road, London WC1 (tel. 01 278 4575).

Patients' Association, 11 Dartmouth Street, London SW1 (tel. 01 222 4922). For complaints about the NHS, and help and advice.

Protection of the Rights of Mental Patients (PROMPT), c/o 2 Boxley House, Pembury Road, London E5 (tel. 01 986 9308).

Publications

American Journal of Pastoral Care, 475 Riverside Drive, New York, NY 10115, USA.

The Association for Pastoral Care and Counselling Journal (address as for the Association).

Contact: the Interdisciplinary Journal of Pastoral Studies, 1 Doune Terrace, Edinburgh EH3 6DY.

Counselling, (address as for the British Association for Counselling).

British Journal of Guidance and Counselling, National Institute for Careers Education and Counselling, Bateman Street, Cambridge CB2 ILZ.

Health and Healing, Churches Council for Health and Healing, St Mary's Vicarage, Ovingham, Prudhoe, Northumberland NE42 6BS.

The Hospital Chaplain (magazine of the Hospital Chaplains Fellowship), Editor, Leavesdon Hospital, College Road, Abbots Langley, Hertfordshire WD5 ONU.

MIND (The National Association for Mental Health), a variety of publications. Address as for MIND.

Index